7 Steps to EFFECTIVE Instructional Leadership

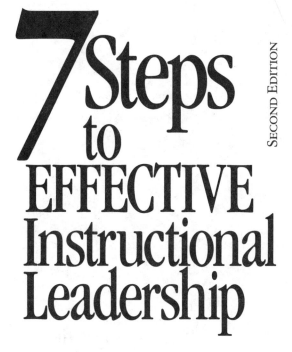

SECOND EDITION

In memory of
James E. Heald, the inspiration for this book
January 3, 1929—September 18, 2001

Elaine K. McEwan

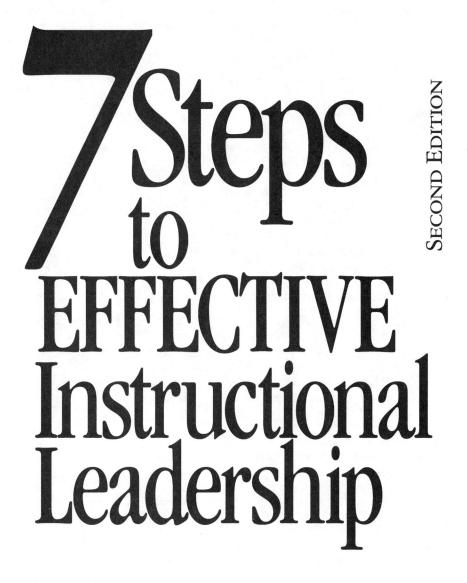

7Steps
to
EFFECTIVE
Instructional
Leadership

SECOND EDITION

CORWIN PRESS, INC.
A Sage Publications Company
Thousand Oaks, California

For information:

Corwin Press, Inc.
A Sage Publications Company
2455 Teller Road
Thousand Oaks, California 91320
www.corwinpress.com

Sage Publications Ltd.
6 Bonhill Street
London EC2A 4PU
United Kingdom

Sage Publications India Pvt. Ltd.
M-32 Market
Greater Kailash I
New Delhi 110 048 India

Printed in the United States of America

Library of Congress Cataloging-in-Publication Data

McEwan, Elaine K., 1941-
   Seven steps to effective instructional leadership / by Elaine
McEwan.— 2nd ed.
       p. cm.
Includes bibliographical references and index.
   ISBN 978-0-7619-4629-8 (c : acid-free paper) — ISBN 978-0-7619-4630-4
(p : acid-free paper)
   1. School principals—Self-rating of—United States. 2. Educational
leadership—United States. 3. Teacher-principal relationships—United
States. I. Title: 7 steps to effective instructional leadership. II. Title.
   LB2831.662 .M34 2002
   371.2'012—dc21
                                                    2002005179

This book is printed on acid-free paper.

08 09 10   7 6 5

Acquisitions Editor:	Robb Clouse
Editorial Assistant:	Erin Clow
Production Editor:	Olivia Weber
Typesetter:	C&M Digitals (P) Ltd.
Indexer:	Michael Ferreira
Cover Designer:	Tracy E. Miller
Production Artist:	Sandra Ng

Contents

Preface

WHAT THIS BOOK IS ABOUT AND WHO SHOULD READ IT

I have been a student of leadership and, more particularly, instructional leadership since the late seventies. Unfortunately, many of the stakeholders in public education have not always shared my enthusiasm regarding its importance. They often seemed oblivious to what is a given in my mind: without an effective principal, forget about having an effective school. Instead, resources across the United States were directed to tests, teachers, and textbooks in an effort to improve student achievement. Standards received far more attention than school leadership, as if a list of outcomes could impact a school without a strong leader at the helm. The debate regarding how best to certify teachers got more press than the critical shortage of outstanding principals. More recently, however, politicians, parents, and even the press are finally giving principals their due. With this renewed interest in and emphasis on the importance of strong instructional leadership in achieving accountable and effective schools, a second edition of *Seven Steps to Effective Instructional Leadership* is timely.

In the fall of 1983, I was hired as the principal of an elementary school in the far western suburbs of Chicago. It was my first principalship, and I was armed with five dress-for-success suits, a newly acquired doctoral degree, and all the answers. Confronted with a student body that was over one third poor and 40 percent minority, standardized achievement test scores that hovered at the 20th percentile, and a staff that seemed powerless in the face of such odds, I discovered that my answers were for a totally different set of questions than those I faced.

I began to search for alternative answers and found them in both expected (the research literature) and unexpected (the collective wisdom of the faculty) places. Research in the early eighties was increasingly demonstrating the impact of building the principal's leadership. But the challenge for me was how to translate that research into action in my own school. I did not have years of experience upon which to draw, and I did not have unlimited staff development funds to train teachers and import new programs. But in my ignorance, I did not realize my limitations. I only knew what I wanted my school to become. That is always the challenge for the principal—how to create a worthy vision and how to motivate and inspire a disparate group of students, teachers, and parents toward that vision. I found that through shared decision making, instructional support and encouragement, and the partnership of businesses in our community, the faculty was energized and empowered. Together we discovered that "the wizard was truly within us."

In the 8 years I served as the principal of that building, student achievement rose dramatically, parental involvement as measured by PTA membership and financial support tripled, and our image in the community turned around. Teachers participated in planning and decision making through a building-leadership team. The faculty came to view their principal as a leader rather than a manager. Decisions were no longer made unilaterally; teachers participated in decision making and were held accountable. Rather than following recipes and rules that were no longer working, we hypothesized, solved problems, and tested new ideas. Teaching was focused on the outcomes we developed together rather than on covering textbooks, and expectations moved from a belief that some can learn to the belief that all can learn. During my 8-year tenure at Lincoln School, I became a student of the instructional leadership literature and dedicated myself to becoming an instructional leader. I constantly monitored and evaluated my own behaviors, and I asked my faculty to share their observations and suggestions with me, both informally and with standardized instruments. In 1989, I was privileged to be named an Instructional Leader by the Illinois Principals Association, and in 1991, I was honored to be named the National Distinguished Principal from Illinois. Above all else, these experiences were humbling since they put me in touch with dozens of exemplary instructional leaders around my state and the country whose accomplishments at leading schools to excellence were awe inspiring. Many of their reflections on instructional leadership are included in the chapters that follow.

I believe that any dedicated educator has the capability to become an exemplary instructional leader. All that one needs is a willingness to learn accompanied by the commitment to follow through in day-to-day behavior. The seven steps to effective instructional leadership that you will read about in the following chapters have been tested by practitioners and validated by research. Adopted, practiced, and refined in your own professional life, they will make a measurable difference in the lives of students, teachers, and parents in your educational community. You will discover that the wizard is truly within you.

WHOM THIS BOOK IS FOR

I have written *Seven Steps to Effective Instructional Leadership* for results-oriented administrators who daily face the pressures of accountability. Effective schools with high-achieving students don't just happen. They are cultivated and thrive under the strong instructional leadership of principals who daily engage in each of the seven steps.

This book is designed for educators in a variety of positions: (a) current school principals who want to renew and revitalize their approach to leadership; (b) prospective principals who need to know how and where to channel their energies in preparing for the principalship; (c) central office administrators who need a template to assist in the hiring, coaching, and evaluation of principals; and (d) university professors who train and mentor current and prospective principals.

OVERVIEW OF THE CONTENTS

The Introduction sets forth the differences between leadership and instructional leadership and defines the critical attributes of effective instructional leadership. Chapters 1 through 7 describe each of the seven steps in detail, set forth explicit behavioral indicators related to each step that will enable you to evaluate yourself and solicit feedback from the teachers with whom you work, and offer practical suggestions from actual principals regarding how they have implemented the seven steps. The book concludes with some immediate things you can do to become an effective instructional leader, a complete Instructional Leadership Checklist, and reproducible response form.

This updated edition of *Seven Steps to Effective Instructional Leadership* contains substantial changes:

- A revision of step one to include standards-based reform, the use of data to drive school improvement, and the necessity for effective instructional leaders to achieve results with their teachers and students
- The addition of personal expectations to step five
- A substantial revision of the Instructional Leadership Checklist along with the inclusion of several new indicators
- An easier-to-use response form that now groups the indicators with their respective steps to effective instructional leadership
- A collection of must-read books to help you extend your learning regarding the seven steps
- Updated references and research

- New vignettes from both elementary and secondary instructional leaders that illustrate how to implement the seven steps to achieve results

ACKNOWLEDGMENTS

I remain indebted to the following individuals who made contributions to the first edition of *Seven Steps to Effective Instructional Leadership.* Many of them have moved from the principalship into central office administration, university teaching, and consulting positions, but they continue to share their instructional leadership expertise with a new generation of both prospective and practicing principals.

To the following instructional leaders who completed lengthy questionnaires or were interviewed or contributed ideas for the first edition, my special thanks. Their insights have enriched my own professional life as well as the pages of this book: Harvey Alvy, Carol Auer, Chuck Baker, James A. Blockinger, Diane Borgman, Dave Burton, Nancy C. Carbone, Amelia Cartrett, Gary Catalani, Maryanne Friend, Nick Friend, Christine Gaylord, Linda Hanson, Robert V. Hassan, Carolyn Hood, Alan Jones, Michael L. Klopfenstein, Brent J. McArdle, Roger Moore, Stella Loeb-Munson, Linda Murphy, Phyllis O'Connell, Ann Parker, Michael Pettibone, Joe Porto, Richard Seyler, Danny Shaw, James D. Shifflet, James J. Simmons, Lynn Sprick, Frances Starks, Merry Gayle Wade, Sister Catherine Wingert, and Paul C. Zaander.

I owe my great and good friend, Don Chase, former field representative for the Illinois Principals Association (IPA), a debt of gratitude for the many opportunities he afforded me to share my ideas with others and grow as an instructional leader. The ink was scarcely dry on my contract when Don was at my door recruiting me to join IPA. It was one of the best decisions I ever made.

The teachers at Lincoln School, West Chicago, Illinois, from 1983 to 1991, taught me most of what I know about instructional leadership. They were unfailingly forthright, long-suffering beyond belief, and showed me on a daily basis that all children *could* learn.

To my former colleague and friend Phyllis O'Connell, who now teaches at North Central College (Illinois), I appreciate her right-brained reading of this manuscript and her extraordinarily creative approach to instructional leadership. Her suggestions and critique were invaluable. Other colleagues who read the manuscript of the first edition and offered assistance were Becky Rosenthal, Tom Giles, John Patterson, and Nancy Coughlin.

My former superintendent John Henning first believed in my abilities, gave me the freedom to grow and change as a person, and enabled me to become an instructional leader. I have learned much from his wise counsel and his example as a leader.

To my late husband, Richard, whose encouragement to write this book did not die when he did, I am grateful.

My final tribute I reserve for my husband and business partner, E. Raymond Adkins, whose love, warmth, patience, gentle spirit, and unerring eye for detail have seen this book from its beginning to the final form.

Two individuals convinced me of the need for a second edition of *Seven Steps to Effective Instructional Leadership* and thoughtfully shared exactly what needed to be added to the book to make it more timely and applicable to both prospective and practicing administrators. Both of these gifted teachers have used the first edition as a textbook in their graduate courses on the principalship and know its contents as well or better than the author: ElizaBeth McCay, assistant professor of educational administration at Virginia Commonwealth University, and Roland Smith, longtime school superintendent and currently professor of educational administration at the University of Arkansas, Fayetteville.

A special thanks to Sandra Ahola, Kathie Dobberteen, Alan Jones, and Yvonne Peck for sharing their expertise with the readers of this second edition. Alan contributed to the first edition, but he is still going strong—eloquent and thought provoking as always. Kathie attended one of my first raising-reading-achievement workshops and went back to her building to turn it upside down with her zeal for making sure that no child left her school without knowing how to read and write on grade level. I have worked with Sandra's staff to improve reading achievement in her K-8 school and have experienced firsthand her effective instructional leadership at work. I first met Yvonne at one of my workshops and was immediately impressed with her passion for achieving results at the high school level. As an assistant principal at this level, she knows the challenge of being an instructional leader in a school of 3,000 students while sitting in the second chair. She always has time for my questions in spite of the demands on her time.

Writing books is often a lonely endeavor, and a phrase from that old cowboy song "Home on the Range" could well be paraphrased to describe the life of an author: "Where seldom is heard an *encouraging* word . . . ." My special thanks to Roland Smith for sending me the following *encouraging* words taken from an answer to a comprehensive examination question written by one of his students. These words, above all else, convinced me to write the second edition of *Seven Steps to Effective Instructional Leadership:*

The fourth priority I would attempt to accomplish in my first year [as a principal] would be to continually practice the seven steps for effective instructional leadership as set out in Elaine McEwan's book of the same title. No other work has influenced the formation of my philosophy more. [The seven steps have] provided me [with] a roadmap for developing what I hope is an effective educational administrative philosophy.

About the Author

**Elaine K. McEwan** is a partner and educational consultant with the McEwan-Adkins Group, which offers workshops and consulting services in instructional leadership, school improvement, raising reading achievement K-12, and school-community relations. A former teacher, media specialist, principal, and assistant superintendent for instruction in a suburban Chicago school district, she is the author of more than two dozen books for parents and educators. Her Corwin titles include *Leading Your Team to Excellence: Making Quality Decisions* (1997); *Seven Steps to Effective Instructional Leadership* (1998); *The Principal's Guide to Attention Deficit Hyperactivity Disorder* (1998); *How to Deal with Parents Who Are Angry, Troubled, Afraid, or Just Plain Crazy* (1998); *The Principal's Guide to Raising Reading Achievement* (1998); *Counseling Tips for Elementary School Principals* (1999) with Jeffrey A. Kottler; *Managing Unmanageable Students: Practical Solutions for Educators* (2000) with Mary Damer; *The Principal's Guide to Raising Math Achievement* (2000); *Raising Reading Achievement in Middle and High Schools: Five Simple-to-Follow Strategies for Principals* (2001); *Ten Traits of Highly Effective Teachers: How to Hire, Mentor, and Coach Successful Teachers* (2001); and *Teach Them ALL to Read: Catching the Kids Who Fall Through the Cracks* (2002).

She is the education columnist for the *Northwest Explorer* newspaper, a contributing author to several online Web sites for parents, and can be heard on a variety of syndicated radio programs helping parents solve schooling problems. She was honored by the Illinois Principals Association as an outstanding instructional leader, by the Illinois State Board of Education with an Award of Excellence in the Those Who Excel Program, and by the National Association of Elementary School Principals as the National Distinguished Principal from Illinois for 1991. She received her undergraduate degree in education from Wheaton College and advanced degrees in library science (MA) and educational administration (EdD) from Northern Illinois University. McEwan lives with her husband and business partner, E. Raymond Adkins, in Oro Valley, Arizona. Visit her Web site at www.elainemcewan.com, where you can learn more about her writing and workshops, or contact her directly at emcewan@elainemcewan.com.

Introduction

Thousands of school buildings dot the landscapes of America. Some have been designed by famous architects and bear historical landmark status. Others are vestiges of the cement block construction that characterized schools built for the burgeoning student population of the late fifties and early sixties. Some school buildings are located in wealthy suburban areas, while still others rise among the shattered dreams of inner-city housing projects. Some serve homogeneous populations; others have hallways that rival the United Nations in diversity. The public earnestly desires and often stridently demands that the adults who occupy these diverse buildings on a daily basis—teachers, administrators, and other support staff—prepare young people for the future; teach children the skills they need to be successful in life; and motivate our youth to read, write, and think creatively. Many schools, irrespective of their physical location or the demographics of the students they serve, accomplish those goals. These schools can be characterized by any number of adjectives— *effective, excellent,* or *outstanding* are three. There are, however, too many schools that can be described in less than flattering terms—*poor, ineffective,* or *just plain mediocre.*

Researchers have long been fascinated with the differences between effective and ineffective schools. The possibility of fixing broken schools or improving mediocre ones by manipulating key variables in the school environment is a tantalizing one for educational reformers. And while each researcher has generated a slightly different set of descriptors that characterize effective or excellent schools, one variable always emerges as critically important: the leadership abilities of the building principal, particularly in the instructional arena. Although the Illinois legislature was prescient enough in the early eighties to mandate that building principals spend at least 51 percent of their time being instructional leaders (and that law is still on the books), many of the movers and shakers in the educational world were somewhat slow to recognize the critical role of the principal in bringing about standards-based reform. Not coincidentally, they were also reluctant to allocate monies for training that included more than just how to manage "buses, budgets, and boilers." Many educational administration programs have eschewed the practical for the theoretical, leaving aspiring principals to train themselves on the job.

A report by Arthur Andersen LLP (1997) made the following recommendation:

> The key factor to the individual school's success is the building principal, who sets the tone as the school's educational leader, enforces the positive, and convinces the students, parents and teachers that all children can learn and improve academically. Our overall assessment is that the school principal has the greatest single impact on student performance. As a result we believe that increased attention and funding needs to be directed towards programs that attract, evaluate, train and retain the best principals. (p. 27)

As educators ushered in the 21st century, a flurry of reports, panels, and initiatives—all focused on a redefinition of the principal's role—made the news (Olson, 2000; Richard, 2000). Among these:

- *Leadership for Student Learning: Reinventing the Principalship* (Institute for Educational Leadership, 2000)
- *The Principal, Keystone of a High-Achieving School: Attracting and Keeping the Leaders We Need* (Educational Research Service, National Association of Elementary School Principals, National Association of Secondary Principals, 2000)
- *Trying to Stay Ahead of the Game: Superintendents and Principals Talk about School Leadership* (Public Agenda, 2001)
- *Priorities and Barriers in High School Leadership: A Survey of Principals* (National Association of Elementary School Principals, 2001)
- *Leading Learning Communities: Standards for What Principals Should Know and Be Able to Do* (National Association of Elementary School Principals, 2001)

All these documents echoed three major themes:

1. The focus of the principalship must be shifted from management to instructional leadership.

2. Instructional leadership is essential to developing and sustaining excellent schools.

3. There is a shortage of trained administrators who are capable of handling the demands of instructional leadership.

Just ahead, we will examine leadership in the broad sense and instructional leadership specifically and then set forth seven steps that can help you respond to the increased attention now focused on your role as an instructional leader.

WHAT IS LEADERSHIP?

Leadership is an endlessly fascinating topic. Sports fans, school board members, stockholders, and academicians all have their theories about what constitutes a leader. Although many well-known definitions of leadership are included in this chapter, the classic one by Tannenbaum, Weschler, and Massarik

> There is nothing more difficult to take in hand, more perilous to conduct, or more uncertain in its success, than to take the lead in the introduction of a new order of things.
>
> (Machiavelli, 1985, p. 23)

(1961) still encompasses the most critical dimensions of leadership: "Interpersonal influence directed through the communication process toward the attainment of some goal or goals" (p. 24). *Defining* leadership has never been a problem for researchers and theorists. Discovering how to create or produce leaders has been somewhat more difficult. The classical theorists debated whether leadership was a function of individuals and their characteristics or whether the historical context served to shape individuals in response to societal needs or events.

Most contemporary researchers, however, have found it far more constructive to study what leaders actually do, rather than to focus on traits like intelligence, friendliness, or creativity. What makes individuals able to lead their organization (business, school, or sports team) to greatness while other individuals—although equally intelligent, friendly, competent, and caring—manage to achieve only mediocrity? What makes some individuals highly effective as leaders in some settings while in others, they are only marginally successful?

> The manager administers; the leader innovates.
> The manager has a short-range view; the leader has a long-range perspective.
> The manager asks how and when; the leader asks what and why.
> The manager accepts the status quo; the leader challenges it.
> The manager does things right; the leader does the right thing.
>
> (Bennis, 1989, p. 45)

Bass (1990) enumerates a variety of characteristics that differentiate leaders from followers:

A strong drive for responsibility and task completion, vigor and persistence in pursuit of goals, venturesomeness and originality in problem solving, the drive to exercise initiative in social situations, self-confidence and sense of personal identity, willingness to accept consequences of decisions and action, readiness to absorb interpersonal stress, willingness to tolerate frustration and delay, the ability to influence other persons' behavior, and the capacity to structure social interaction systems to the purpose at hand. (p. 81)

> The leader is a person who is in a position to influence others to act and who has, as well, the moral, intellectual, and social skills required to take advantage of that position.
>
> (Schlechty, 1990, p. xix)

Some theorists have hypothesized that effective leaders not only possess many of these characteristics, but they also are able to match their leadership styles to the unique needs of the situation. Rather than behaving in the same way in every setting, effective leaders assess the situation and adjust their leadership behaviors to the complexity of the tasks or goals as well as the composition and characteristics of the groups they are leading (Blanchard, Zigarmi, & Zigarmi, 1985).

Bennis and Nanus (1985) enlarged the definition of leadership to include more than just managing, defining managers as people who do things right and leaders as people who do the right thing, while Peters and Austin (1985) tinkered still further with the definition of leadership. They proposed that the model of manager as "cop, referee, devil's advocate, dispassionate analyst, professional decision-maker, naysayer, and pronouncer" be put to rest and that the model of leader as "cheerleader, enthusiast, nurturer of champions, hero finder, wanderer, dramatist, coach, facilitator, and builder" (p. 265) replace it. For sheer succinctness, however, nothing surpasses former NASSP executive director Scott Thomson's (Kelly, 1980) definition of leadership as "getting the job done through people" (p. v).

Leadership models have traditionally been developed and tested in the business world or sports arenas, and there have been more than 100 books written in the past 20 years from these two perspectives, each proposing a slightly different leadership paradigm (Schwahn & Spady, 1998). Educators are sometimes made to feel that without the vision of Wal-Mart founder Sam Walton, the charisma of business executive Jack Welch, or the team-building efficiency of college basketball coaches Rick Pitino and Pat Summit, we are doomed to failure. Success in the business world, however, can be measured in terms of bottom lines, increased productivity and sales, and rises in stock prices, while coaches get points for winning seasons. Educators, particularly principals, face a different set of challenges. Although many of the lessons of leadership in the corporate or sports world are quite applicable within the walls of our schools, we need our own model of leadership, one that incorporates the unique characteristics of education and "places student and adult learning at the center of schools" (National Association of Elementary School Principals, 2001, p. 3). The challenges of *instructional leadership* require a somewhat different leadership paradigm.

HOW DOES INSTRUCTIONAL LEADERSHIP DIFFER?

The emphasis placed on the leadership role of the principal has changed dramatically during the past 30 years. An assignment given to the typical graduate student in educational administration in the seventies or early eighties was to develop a list of jobs in the seven traditional administrative task areas (staff personnel, pupil personnel, school-community, instructional and curriculum development, finance and business management, facilities management, and intergovernmental agency relations) as they relate to the four classic management functions (planning, organizing, leading, and controlling). Today's administrator-in-training must major in instructional leadership, learning how to fulfill essential management functions through skillful delegation and collaboration while excelling in creating a learning community.

Sergiovanni (1984, 1991) proposed one of the earliest models of instructional leadership. He first identified five leadership forces: (a) technical, (b) human, (c) educational, (d) symbolic, and (e) cultural. The technical aspects of instructional leadership deal with the traditional practices of management, the topics such as planning, time management, leadership theory, and organizational development that are usually covered in an administrative theory course. The human component encompasses all the interpersonal aspects of leadership: communicating, motivating, and facilitating. The technical and human leadership skills, according to Sergiovanni, are generic. They are not unique to schools and should be present in any organization where strong leadership is evident. Effective leaders, regardless of the setting, need planning and time-management skills as well as the ability to organize and coordinate. Whether the team players are teachers, engineers, or point guards, the effective leader needs to be skilled in providing support and encouragement, helping to build consensus and interpersonal communication. These qualities are givens for any successful leader.

It is the remaining leadership forces—educational, symbolic, and cultural—that are specific to the school setting and constitute instructional leadership. The educational force involves all the instructional aspects of the principal's role—teaching, learning, and curriculum. The symbolic and cultural forces derive from the instructional leader's abilities to represent the school and what is important and purposeful about the school (symbolic) as well as the ability to articulate the values and beliefs of the organization over time (cultural).

> Instructional leadership is leadership that is directly related to the processes of instruction where teachers, learners, and the curriculum interact.
>
> (Acheson & Smith, 1986, p. 3)

Instructional leaders must be knowledgeable about learning theory, effective instruction, and curriculum—the power within the educational force. In addition, instructional leaders must be able to communicate and represent to students, teachers, and parents what is of import and value in the school. They must become a symbolic force. Finally, instructional leaders must be skilled in the actual construction of a culture that specifically defines what a given school is all about. The educational, symbolic, and cultural dimensions are critical to leadership in the *school* setting.

Sergiovanni (2001) has more recently subsumed the educational, symbolic, and cultural leadership forces described in this earlier model of the principalship into a new theory of school leadership—one that focuses on the school as a community and the principal as a servant:

> Servant leadership describes well what it means to be a principal. Principals are responsible for "ministering" to the needs of the schools they serve. The needs are defined by the shared values and purposes of the school's covenant. They minister by furnishing help and being of service to parents, teachers and students. They minister by providing leadership in a way that encourages others to be leaders in their own right. They minister by highlighting and protecting the values of the school. The principal as minister is one who is devoted to a cause, mission, or set of ideas and accepts the duty and obligation to serve this cause. (pp. 357-358)

Sister Catherine Wingert,[1] principal of St. Dorothy's School in Chicago, is a true servant leader in the highest sense of the word: "Instructional leadership is the creation of a climate where the principal, faculty, students, parents, and school board are able to work together to accomplish the task of education."

When queried about their responsibilities, instructional leaders rarely, if ever, note the ability to use time wisely or manage the day-to-day operations of a building, seeing these qualities as givens but, rather, focused on vision, communication, risk-taking, and commitment:

An instructional leader has a sense of purpose and a broad knowledge of the educational process and learning theories. She's a risk taker, and has people skills and unlimited energy. (Frances Stark)

An instructional leader has a passion for great teaching and a vision for what schools should be doing for children. He should have well-thought-out answers for three fundamental questions about schooling: How do children learn? How should we teach children? And how should we treat subject matter? (Alan Jones)

A very practical description of instructional leadership can be found in *Leading Learning Communities: Standards for What Principals Should Know and Be Able to Do* (National Association of Elementary School Principals, 2001). It sets forth six standards of instructional leadership that are unequivocal and nonnegotiable in their focus on learning.

1. Lead schools in a way that places student and adult learning at the center.

2. Set high expectations and standards for the academic and social development of all students and the performance of adults.

3. Demand content and instruction that ensure student achievement of agreed-on academic standards.

4. Create a culture of continuous learning for adults tied to student learning and other school goals.

5. Use multiple sources of data as diagnostic tools to assess, identify, and apply instructional improvement.

6. Actively engage the community to create shared responsibility for student and school success. (pp. 6-7)

WHAT DOES THE RESEARCH TELL US?

Research has a great deal to say about the importance of instructional leadership with regard to its impact on school effectiveness and ultimately on student achievement. There are several different perspectives from which to study the subject (Northwest Educational Cooperative, 1985; Northwest Regional Educational Laboratory, 1984):

Schools operated by principals who were perceived by their teachers to be strong instructional leaders exhibited significantly greater gain scores in achievement in reading and mathematics than did schools operated by average and weak instructional leaders.

(Andrews & Soder, 1987, p. 9)

1. *School effectiveness* research: What kind of schoolwide practices help students learn, and what role does the principal play in the interaction and creation of these practices?

2. *Principal effectiveness* research: What are the most important characteristics of effective principals?

3. *Instructional leadership* research: What practices of principals promote and support teaching and learning?

4. *Organizational change* research: How can principals promote significant and lasting change in their schools?

5. *Teacher effects* research: What instructional practices are most effective in bringing about student learning?

6. *Curriculum alignment* research: What are the best ways to organize and manage curriculum?

7. *Program coupling* research: How does the interaction of practices in the district, school, and classrooms impact student learning?

While any given research study or body of research taken in isolation might be uneven in terms of quality, or fail to present a completely conclusive finding, when taken as a total body of work, all these research bases clearly support the critical importance of the principal as instructional leader. The responsibility for what is happening with regard to teaching and learning in each of the schools across America on a daily basis clearly falls on the shoulders of the building principal.

But how can a mere mortal principal be expected to digest, synthesize, evaluate, and put into practice on a daily basis all the findings contained in the more than 200 studies cited in the references just mentioned? "Just tell me what to do," replies the beleaguered principal beset by discipline problems, budget deficits, and broken-down boilers.

Persell and Cookson (1982) assisted practitioners by reviewing and synthesizing more than 75 studies. They reported that strong principals exhibit the following behaviors:

- They demonstrate a commitment to academic goals.
- They create a climate of high expectations.
- They function as instructional leaders.
- They are forceful and dynamic as leaders.
- They consult effectively with others.
- They create order and discipline.
- They marshal resources.

- They use time well.
- They evaluate their results.

Rutherford (1985) narrowed the list still further to four behaviors that differentiated effective principals from less-effective ones. Effective principals:

- Have "clear informed visions of what they want their schools to become—visions that focus on students and their needs."
- "Translate these visions into goals for their schools and expectations for their teachers, students and administrators."
- Do not stand back and wait for things to happen, but "continuously monitor progress."
- "Intervene in a supportive or corrective manner when this seems necessary." (p. 32)

Early research on the impact of strong instructional leadership on student achievement came from Andrews and Soder (1987). Rather than merely describing instructional leadership behavior, they sought to show how this behavior impacted the performance of students, particularly low-achieving students. They administered questionnaires to teachers in the 67 elementary schools and 20 secondary schools of the Seattle, Washington, school district. Eighteen different interactions that occur between principals and teachers were measured in four key areas: the principal as resource provider, the principal as instructional resource, the principal as communicator, and the principal as visible presence. Their findings showed that the normal equivalent-gain scores of students in schools led by strong instructional leaders (as perceived by the teachers in those schools) were significantly greater in both total reading and total mathematics than those of students in schools rated as having average or weak leaders (as perceived by the teachers in those schools).

More recently, Hallinger and Heck (1996), in a synthesis of 15 years of research on how principals impact their schools, concluded that principals exercise a *measurable*, though indirect, effect on school effectiveness and student achievement. About the *indirect* aspect, they write: "The fact that leadership effects on school achievement appear to be indirect is neither cause for alarm or dismay. [A]chieving results through others is the essence of leadership" (p. 39).

In a report prepared for the National Association of Elementary School Principals and the National Association of Secondary School Principals by the Educational Research Service (2000), the authors concluded that the impact of principal leadership on student achievement is a compelling one: if you want to have an effective school characterized by teachers and students who are dedicated to learning, become a strong instructional leader. But how?

CAN ANY PRINCIPAL BECOME AN INSTRUCTIONAL LEADER?

> Nurture is far more important than nature in determining who becomes a successful leader. . . . Learning to be a leader is somewhat like learning to be a parent or a lover; your childhood and adolescence provide you with basic values and role models.
>
> (Bennis & Nanus, 1985, p. 223)

There is no magic recipe or failure-proof formula that can deliver instant instructional leadership. Even though you are reading a book that offers seven steps to effective instructional leadership, there is no money-back guarantee or promise of future success. The mere reading of this book (or any other) will not turn you into Superleader overnight. The seven steps must be combined with training, time, hard work, painful setbacks, passionate dedication, and commitment.

Chris Gaylord's staff found her to be a "strong instructional leader," using the same instrument Andrews and Soder (1987) used in their study to identify strong versus weak instructional leaders. Based on her own experience, she believes that:

> [Any educator can be an instructional leader] if he or she wants to and possesses some basic talents and education. I can say this because I had no idea I'd *become* a principal! I was recruited and groomed and encouraged and supported. Both administration and staff cared enough to give me feedback along with the essentials of a vision until I could carry it on and help develop it myself.

Carol Auer served as an award-winning elementary principal for more than a decade and is now a central office administrator. She believes that all you need to become a strong instructional leader is *ganas*—a Spanish word she learned from her Hispanic students, meaning that often-indefinable will or desire.

Gary Catalani, a former high school principal and now school superintendent who has presented workshops on instructional leadership, believes that practical experience is critical: "Instructional leadership is a development process. One can't be trained to be an instructional leader. Through course work and on-the-job learning experiences one can develop into an instructional leader."

Alan Jones doesn't mince any words about the demands of becoming a strong instructional leader: "To be an instructional leader, you must be a person who eats and sleeps teaching and learning. Instructional leaders must constantly think about how to organize a school and instruction so all children can learn."

Nick and Mary Ann Friend are a dynamic duo. Between them they have more than three decades in elementary and middle school principalships. Their staff members identified both of them as strong instructional leaders. This is their cooperative response to the question of what it takes to become an effective instructional leader:

> A person must believe in the capabilities of others and must be able to communicate this belief to others. He/she must be able to recognize what needs to be done and the best way to do it. He/she must be able to create a trust relationship, explain his/her vision/goal and empower others. In addition he/she must be willing to plan, prioritize, and spend all the time necessary to be an instructional leader.

WHAT ARE THE BARRIERS TO BECOMING AN EFFECTIVE INSTRUCTIONAL LEADER?

Although the research clearly shows that instructional leadership behaviors make a difference, how do practicing principals measure up in their demonstration of these behaviors? In a survey of 250 principals, Ames (1989) reported these discouraging results. Forty percent of the principals surveyed seldom or never discussed school goals with students. Thirty-six percent seldom or never recognized teaching at formal ceremonies. Half of them seldom or never modeled effective teaching techniques, and over one third seldom or never helped teachers develop strategies for good teaching. Almost one fourth of the principals surveyed said they seldom or never discussed assessment results with faculty. Even more dismaying than the responses of the principals themselves are the discrepancies reported between the principals' perceptions of themselves and teachers' perceptions. When asked if they spent time supervising teaching, nearly half of the principals responded in the affirmative. Teachers reported that only 30 percent of the principals did it. When asked if they spent time managing curriculum, nearly three fourths of the principals answered yes. Teachers thought the percentage was less than half.

There is a wide gap between the ideal and the actual behaviors of principals as described in this survey data—suggesting some significant barriers to principals actually doing on a daily basis what is most effective in achieving results in America's schools.

Lack of Skills and Training

While many universities are restructuring their administration programs to provide more opportunities to develop leadership skills in addition to academic knowledge, a gap remains between the academe and the real world. We cannot, however, bury our heads and blame our lack of skills on anyone else. Those who want to become instructional leaders must seek out training and development opportunities through networking with colleagues, professional organizations, and personal programs of self-improvement (Educational Research Service, 2000, pp. 46-75).

Lack of Teacher Cooperation

Collective bargaining is a fact of life in most large urban and suburban school districts. Contracts are often written specifically to protect teachers from their principals' intrusion on instructional and curricular decisions, making it difficult for instructional leaders to engage in the kind of collaborative discussion, planning, and problem solving regarding instruction that are essential if schools are to improve (Fink & Resnick, 2001). After all, the question goes, "What does he know about teaching third grade? He was a middle school science teacher." "How can she give me feedback on teaching chemistry? She was a music teacher."

Distrustful attitudes on the part of teachers often serve to distance their inexperienced principals who, feeling unprepared to talk teaching with a veteran, opt instead to do what they know how to do best— "administrivia." This reticence to visit classrooms informally soon becomes a habit until principals know little or nothing about what is happening instructionally in their schools.

On the other hand, strong instructional leaders (or those who aspire to be) become learners themselves—attending curriculum training programs along with their teachers, teaching lessons to students, seeking out master teachers from whom to learn, and identifying mature instructional leaders to shadow on the job. Although the message, "I'm the principal and I'm here to help you," may initially be received like its humorous counterpart, "I'm from the government, and I'm here to help you," strong instructional leaders do everything they can to break down the barriers.

Lack of Time

Every school principal operates within the same time constraints. There are never enough hours in the day. The Public Agenda (2001) poll, mentioned earlier in the chapter, surveyed 909 principals regarding various aspects of their job and concluded that if instructional leadership was to be a priority, "[it] must contend with the overcrowded agenda that so many school leaders appear to already face" (p. 11). A similar study by the National Association of Secondary School Principals (2001) found that 70 percent of the respondents considered lack of time as the biggest hurdle in their work. Additional responsibilities are continually added, and nothing is taken away. This layering creates a sense of frustration and impotence that was described by one administrator as the "gerbil on a treadmill syndrome"—going around and around and getting nowhere (Portin & Williams, 1996).

One of the major differences between average principals and strong instructional leaders is how they choose to use the time they *do* have available. Average principals become consumed with management and administrivia. Strong instructional leaders focus on learning. They delegate, facilitate, and collaborate to maximize the amount of time they have available to focus on instructional issues. They recognize the necessity for developing systems and routines that reduce both paperwork and reinventing the wheel. They delegate authority and share responsibility in order to maximize their efficiency. They carefully prioritize how their valuable time is spent and are able to say no to activities and tasks that do not contribute to the instructional mission of the school. Strong principals hire outstanding office, maintenance, and auxiliary personnel; hold high expectations for their performance; and convey to these individuals the key roles they play in supporting the instructional program.[2] They hire the most effective teachers they can find, ensuring that their valuable time can be used for mentoring and coaching—not evaluating and terminating. Strong instructional leaders communicate to parents and community members the priority of instructional leadership in the principal's calendar and train office personnel how to protect and promote classroom observation and instructional priorities for the principal. They learn how to say no to trivial pursuits and take the pithy advice of Labovitz and Rosansky (1997): "The main thing, is to keep the main thing, the main thing!" (p. 3). Every principal has the same amount of available time. Strong instructional leaders use this time to develop and maintain vibrant learning communities rather than to push papers and promote programs.

Lack of Support From Superintendents, School Boards, and Community

The frustration and discouragement of some principals regarding the real or perceived lack of support from those around them is clearly a barrier to becoming an instructional leader.

I go almost every year to conventions for principals, and there's always a speech telling us we need to be education leaders not managers. It's a great idea. And yet the system doesn't easily allow you to be an educational leader. Everyone wants the power to run schools in one way or another—the central office, the union, the board, the parents, the special-interest groups. What's left for the principal to decide isn't always very much. There's so little we have to control or to change. The power, the authority, is somewhere else, though not necessarily the responsibility. (Boyer, 1983, p. 219)

Seventy percent of the principals surveyed by Public Agenda (2001) reported that "managing harsh public criticism and political heat has become a routine part of their job" (p. 9).

Many of the instructional leaders with whom I spoke faced obstacles when they accepted their first principalships: colleagues that were skeptical or intimidated by their strong beliefs and determination, budgets that were diminished by dwindling resources, schools that were demoralized by low-achievement scores, unruly students, iron-clad teacher contracts that stymied creativity and individual responsibility, and ineffective teachers who seemed powerless to change. But these principals jumped the hurdles, destroyed the arguments, maneuvered around the obstacles, cajoled the naysayers, and achieved the unimaginable. Strong instructional leaders have the ability to visualize what a school should be and can become and, somehow, do not permit themselves to be hamstrung by what others may perceive as barriers.

Lack of Vision, Will, or Courage

Lack of vision, will, and courage are the biggest barriers to becoming instructional leaders. We are our own worst enemies. But with vision, will, and courage, any principal can become an instructional leader. The message from successful instructional leaders is this: All of us can be instructional leaders if we:

1. Have vision

2. Have the knowledge base

3. Are willing to take risks

4. Are willing to put in long hours

5. Are willing to accept constructive feedback

6. Are willing to change and grow constantly

7. Thrive on change and ambiguity

8. Can empower others

WHAT ARE THE SEVEN STEPS
TO EFFECTIVE INSTRUCTIONAL LEADERSHIP?

The Seven Steps to Effective Instructional Leadership are neither new nor revolutionary. They are variations on the critical themes that have been presented throughout this introduction:

1. Establish, implement, and achieve academic standards.

2. Be an instructional resource for your staff.

3. Create a school culture and climate conducive to learning.

4. Communicate the vision and mission of your school.

5. Set high expectations for your staff and yourself.

6. Develop teacher leaders.

7. Develop and maintain positive relationships with students, staff, and parents.

While the seven steps cover familiar ground, what is unusual is the approach I have taken to help you integrate each of these steps into your own repertoire of behaviors on a daily basis. The problem with most descriptions of instructional leadership is their failure to define the attributes or characteristics in specific behavioral terms that principals can understand and use. Telling principals they need to communicate the mission of their schools to everyone in the school community is too vague. Are they to take out advertisements in the local paper or hire a skywriter? Principals need to know how that statement can be translated into action on Monday morning. Research tells us that strong instructional leaders set clear instructional goals. But what does that look like in actual practice? The experts tell us that we should be a visible presence. Sounds a little mysterious and otherworldly until you enumerate concrete ways in which successful principals achieve that goal. Each of these steps will be discussed in Chapters 1 through 7 where you will find:

- Detailed but easy-to-read descriptions of each of the seven steps
- Reflections from instructional leaders on the meaning and importance of the seven steps in their principalships
- An Instructional Leadership Checklist that describes in behavioral terms just what effective instructional leaders do every day in their schools
- Vignettes written by and about several exceptional instructional leaders from both secondary and elementary schools, whose

talents have transformed challenging schools into learning communities

- A list of must-read books for each of the steps to widen your understanding

The Instructional Leadership Checklist is made up of 30 different indicators, several for each of the seven steps. Depending on your current job role, you can use the checklist in a variety of ways: (a) to self-assess your present level of instructional leadership, (b) to gain information from all or selected members of your faculty with regard to their perceptions of your instructional leadership, (c) to help you set goals for improving your instructional leadership, (d) to help you evaluate progress toward meeting the goal of becoming a true instructional leader, or (e) to assist a principal-in-training or a principal-in-trouble to develop instructional leadership skills. You can use all or parts of the checklist, depending on your own personal progress toward becoming an effective instructional leader.

The checklist does not prescribe methodologies or improvement models. Your school may be doing site-based management, cooperative learning, block scheduling, or Success for All (Slavin & Madden, 2001). It may be an Accelerated School (Accelerated Schools Project, 2002), an Essential School (Coalition of Essential Schools, 2002), a Comer School (Comer School Development Program, 2002), or an Edison School (Edison Schools, 2002). As Deal (1986) points out,

> Each approach has a cadre of gurus, scholars, advocates, and disciples who righteously defend one view against criticism from other camps. The end result is a cacophony of voices: a dialogue of the deaf among academics, usually a source of confusion among those struggling with how to improve schools. (p. 115)

Becoming an instructional leader is, however, a goal that can be accomplished in the context of any instructional or organizational model. This is not another layer of prescriptions. Remember that implementing the seven steps to effective instructional leadership is not something you will do to your school or teachers but something you will do to yourself. You as a person are going to change the way you go about doing business. You will focus less on changing others and more on letting others respond to the changes you make in your own behavior. You need no one's permission to implement the seven steps. They do not cost anything or require expensive consultants. You need not even tell anyone that you are doing something different. But do not be surprised when parents, students, teachers, and even your superintendent begin to notice. The changes you make in your own behavior will produce dramatic results in the effectiveness of your teachers, the learning of your students, the support of your parents and community, and the personal satisfaction you will feel from having made a difference.

NOTES

1. I am indebted to the many highly effective instructional leaders who shared their opinions, reflections, ideas, and dreams about the principalship with me. Their words bring the seven steps of effective instructional leadership to life. Nearly every individual who made a contribution is identified by name. They completed questionnaires, talked with me personally, sent emails, shared official documents, and, in some cases, even contributed personal reflections. To save the busy reader time, I have omitted individual citations for these quotations unless they have appeared in a published work or an official document that is included in the References.

2. I recently phoned a school and asked to speak with the principal. The secretary replied, "He's here somewhere. I'm not really sure what he's doing." This kind of response leaves a question in the mind of the caller regarding the effectiveness and efficiency of the principal. In a similar phone call to another school, I received this response: "Mr. Jones is out in the building visiting classrooms this morning. May I have him call you later?"

Step One:
Establish,
Implement,
and Achieve
Academic Standards

If the primary purpose of schooling is learning, then determining what students need to know, how and when it should be taught, and whether or not these instructional goals have been reached are paramount for effective instructional leaders. Decisions about what to teach were easy when textbooks *were* the curriculum. Principals could place one teacher's edition and 30 books for each course or subject in the hands of the teacher and depart, confident that the material was being covered. However, establishing instructional goals for the 21st century is a far more daunting assignment. The National Research Council (2000) has framed the following important questions that need to be asked and answered by instructional leaders and their staff members:

> To provide a knowledge-centered classroom environment, attention must be given to what is taught (information, subject matter), why it is taught (understanding), and what competence or mastery looks like.
>
> (Bransford, Brown, & Cocking, 2000, p. 24)

- What specific knowledge and skills should all students learn?
- How do we decide what is in or out of the curriculum?
- Should all students learn the same content, or should it differ for those with different aspirations, abilities, and interests?
- If we agree that we want students to have more than a temporary acquaintance with important concepts and skills, how do we

modify the curriculum so that there is adequate time for in-depth learning?

- How do we assess that kind of learning?
- How do we incorporate the growing body of research that indicates that the most-effective teaching strategies are highly content-specific—that content and instruction are inseparable—into our decision making?

HOW CAN YOU ESTABLISH MEANINGFUL ACADEMIC STANDARDS?

> Defining school goals is a process of balancing clear academic ideals with community and internal school needs. A leader provides the guidance and central themes for this orchestration of goals, from the unit objectives to the general understanding of a school's philosophy.
>
> (Weber, 1987, p. 6)

Instructional leaders are ultimately responsible for guiding the establishment, implementation, and assessment of a set of clear instructional goals or standards for their schools—broad general outcomes that define what students should know and be able to do when they exit the school. In addition to these broad goals in every curricular area and for every grade level, teachers also need specific benchmarks to guide their daily lesson planning. These more discrete outcomes will constitute the road map for learning that teachers will follow. This road map will guide the selection of materials and programs (curriculum), dictate the types of instructional strategies and approaches that are used (pedagogy), and suggest the kinds of formative assessments (both informal and standardized) needed to determine if students are making adequate progress toward achieving the standards.

> Standards provide all parents, teachers, and students in a state with clear expectations of what all students should learn. They also contribute to coherent educational practices when teachers align their instructional methods and materials with assessments based on these standards.
>
> (Stotsky, 2000, p. iii)

Many districts and schools no longer have the freedom to choose what their teachers will teach or how and when their students will be assessed. Most states have developed academic standards and administer periodic assessments in every curricular area and at most grade levels. This fact of educational life in the 21st century drives our instructional efforts and is most assuredly a mixed blessing, for all standards and their concomitant assessments are *not* created equal. If a standard is fuzzy, indefinite, or incapable of being evaluated, as many current standards are, most teachers will ignore them or substitute learning outcomes of their own choosing. A teacher-selected set of outcomes may or may not be articulated and connected highly content-specific with any other teacher's chosen standards. A verbose or repetitive standards document invites teachers to tuck it away on a shelf to gather dust rather than to consult it daily as a road map for where to head next. Some teachers may profess adherence to the standards but fail to prioritize instruction or bring lower-achieving students to mastery in the essential outcomes before moving on to cover more material.

Strong instructional leaders work with teachers to translate fuzzy standards into plain English so they have detailed and understandable directions for instruction and communicate with both staff and students to explain the relevance and importance of assessments.

> An authentic assessment system has to be based on known, clear, public, nonarbitrary standards and criteria.
>
> (Wiggins, 1993, p. 51)

Effective instructional leaders facilitate the translation, consolidation, coordination, and integration of state and district standards into a coherent set of school-level marching orders. Some principals even publish an abbreviated version of their school standards in a booklet for parents or develop Goals at a Glance summaries for teachers to keep them focused on the essential outcomes for their grade or subject. Only when teachers take personal ownership of the standards at their grade levels or in their disciplines will they be able to translate them into effective instruction and solid learning for all their students. If used creatively, well-developed standards documents can be a powerful tool for bringing about instructional and curricular change in a school. Rather than bemoaning their limitations or ignoring their mandates, effective instructional leaders use them as leverage to improve instruction and increase student learning.

The standards aren't the only aspect of standards-based reform that pose a challenge to principals. If state assessments measure only basic skills or are unreasonably difficult for all but the highest-achieving students, neither teachers nor students will take them seriously. Strong instructional leaders must respond in several ways: (a) Work with state officials and politicians to ensure that assessments are valid, reliable, and equitable; (b) work with parents and students to help them understand the importance of assessments, not only to the individual student but also to the school and district as a whole; (c) work with teachers to help them design instruction that includes the skills and knowledge students will need to be successful on standards-based assessments.

HOW CAN YOU ENSURE A CONSISTENT AND COHERENT PROGRAM?

A *consistent* program has similar outcomes and curriculum at every grade level (elementary school) or in every content area (secondary school). If a program is inconsistent, it will be characterized by the doing-my-own-thing syndrome. On the other hand, if a consistent program is in place, all students will have the same opportunities to learn. For example, students enrolled in freshman English with Mrs. Bequeath will encounter the same expectations regarding the quantity and quality of text they read and write as the students enrolled in Mr. Smith's section across the hall.

A *coherent* program is connected from the beginning (kindergarten) to the end (12th grade). In a coherent program, preparation for the third-grade assessment does not begin with a mad dash for the finish line at the beginning of third grade, but at the beginning of kindergarten. When coherence is present, teachers at every grade level know the expectations for students in both the preceding and succeeding school years. Ensuring that school and classroom activities are consistent with adopted and mandated standards as well as consistent and coherent with other grade levels or courses in their school necessitates a great deal of planning, collaboration, and cooperation by principals. In some cases, teachers may have to give up their treasured creativity and autonomy with regard to choosing what they will teach and when they will teach it. When that fails to happen, you will be there to ask the difficult questions as well as provide support and encouragement for finding solutions. Here are some ways effective instructional leaders get the job done.

• Put teams of teachers together and provide time for them to solve grade-level or departmental achievement problems. The peer pressures that marginal teachers will feel relative to measuring up to the school mission and mastery of specific outcomes for their students will encourage them to seek out resources and alternative instructional strategies. Let teacher power

---

A FOCUS ON CONTINUOUS IMPROVEMENT: KATHIE DOBBERTEEN, PRINCIPAL

La Mesa Dale Elementary School, La Mesa, California

Kathie Dobberteen, the principal of La Mesa Dale Elementary School, has seamlessly integrated the first of the seven steps to effective instructional leadership into the fabric of her school. Her focus on continuous assessment and improvement has resulted in remarkable gains in student achievement. La Mesa Dale has been named a California Distinguished School, a Title I Distinguished School, and received one of six annual Change Awards from the Chase Manhattan Bank and Fordham University. In the spring of 2001, 90 percent of the students were reading at and above grade level at this Title I school (up from 42 percent in 1996). Ninety-four percent of the fifth graders went on to middle school reading at and above grade level, with 33 percent of them reading at 8th- and 9th-grade levels. There is a sense of academic press and instructional relentlessness at La Mesa Dale that leaves no child behind.

We challenge ourselves and our students to succeed by writing schoolwide goals every year. These goals are

(continued)

assist you in improving the marginal teacher.

- Set schoolwide as well as grade-level, team, or departmental goals. No one will want to be left behind. What you (and your faculty) choose to pay attention to, what you (and your faculty) think is important, and what you (and your faculty) measure and monitor will be accomplished (or begin to be accomplished) more effectively than it ever was in the past.

HOW CAN YOU ENSURE A SCHOOLWIDE FOCUS ON ACHIEVEMENT AND CONTINUOUS IMPROVEMENT?

La Mesa Dale Elementary School
(continued)

directly related to the district's goals, and we solicit input from the School Site Council, the PTA, and surveys of the parent community. Then, each grade level writes its own specific goals based on the school and district goals. These grade level goals are almost always stated in terms of how they can be measured using data and are posted on the bulletin board outside our Parent Center. The heading on the bulletin board says: "We've come so far . . . but we're not satisfied yet!" (K. Dobberteen, 2001, p. 4)

If your goal is student learning, how will you know you have reached your goals? Who will be responsible for charting the course? Focus on data. Look for proof. Insist on results. Involve everyone. The research is clear about the power of the continuous monitoring of progress in bringing about increased student learning (Northwest Regional Educational Laboratory, 1984). Here are some ways that effective instructional leaders collect and use data to drive school improvement.

[The] litmus test for a good school is not its innovations but rather the solid, purposeful, enduring results it tries to obtain for its students.

(Glickman, 1993, p. 50)

- Use test results, grade reports, attendance records, and other information to spot potential problems. Become skilled at picking up bits and pieces of information as you talk with teachers, attendance clerks, counselors, or deans. Move in on potential instructional or learning problems swiftly. Never wait and see when a child's academic success is at stake.

- Use a standardized set of questions every time you approach a data set such as the following: (a) What do these data seem to tell us? (b) What do they not tell us? (c) What else would we need to know? (d) What good news is here for us to celebrate? (e) What needs for school improvement might arise from these data? (Holcomb, 1999, p. 64)

- No matter who teaches a specified course and grade level or what methodologies are used, the outcomes must be consistent. Facilitate the development of common final examinations in core courses or curriculum-based assessments in reading, writing, and mathematics at the elementary school level. These assessments will give teachers a focus, result in better test construction, and enable you, the instructional leader, to monitor the consistency in your curriculum.

> To increase student learning, approach it directly, and bring the energy of everyone in the school or district to bear on the effort.
>
> (Joyce & Showers, 1995, p. 55)

- Share summaries of individual students' performance with all the staff who can then assist in developing action alternatives. *All* the teachers in your school are responsible for all the students. The kindergarten teachers should be interested in the achievement of sixth graders and vice versa. Teachers of graduating seniors should feel as responsible for sophomore course outlines and content as they do for their own syllabi. Work to eliminate the closed-door syndrome characterized by too many teachers who feel no responsibility for what is happening in other classrooms of the building.

- Target low- or underachieving students in your school for an all-out team effort to improve their achievement. Make the target students the responsibility of all faculty members. Form a problem-solving, student-study team to come up with innovative instructional strategies to help these students. Find ways to offer extra help and increased opportunities for success.

> Historically, schools and school systems would be re-accredited and even receive public acclaim if they had the appropriate mix of inputs (books in the library) and curricular offerings (advanced math courses). Unfortunately, these input assessments never addressed the question of how much students were actually learning at the school.
>
> (Lezotte, 1992, p. 58)

- Collect trend data so that you can evaluate your progress over several years. Learn to use spreadsheets and develop databases or hire a secretary who is a whiz so that multiple measures of student achievement are readily available.

- Collect data from other sources in addition to student achievement. Use the level of staff development participation, staff attendance records, parental involvement in PTA, number of school volunteers and the time they volunteer, and the attendance at parent-school activities.

- Survey the faculty, community, and student body relative to their perceptions about the school's effectiveness.

- If your community or state does not issue a report card on student achievement, publish your own school report card so that parents are aware of your emphasis on accountability. Communicate student progress to parents—through published documents, parent conferences, narratives, and portfolios that give a holistic picture of student strengths and weaknesses.

- Match your assessments to standards and do your best to coordinate your school-, district-, and state-level assessments to minimize the amount of time spent in testing.

- Disaggregate different categories of data to determine if all students have an equal chance of achieving academic success in your school. *Disaggregation* is the process of separating out different types of information for different groups of students (e.g., "Do a higher percentage of boys score in the upper quartiles in math and science than girls?" Or "Are specific ethnic groups overrepresented in the lower quartiles on standardized achievement tests?"). Types of data that can be disaggregated include norm-referenced test scores, criterion-referenced test scores, state-level test scores, grade distributions, attendance or tardiness patterns, graduation rates, expulsions, students accepted in postsecondary education programs, graduates placed in jobs, students participating in extracurricular activities, students receiving academic awards and scholarships, discipline referrals, suspensions, advanced-placement enrollments, specific courses (e.g., algebra), and honor roll. Student groups to pull out for comparison might include higher- or lower-socioeconomic status; minority or nonminority; gender; student mobility; or students enrolled in special programs such as Title I, special education, and bilingual education.

- Update student records in a timely fashion so that all the individuals who work with students will have relevant information at their fingertips.

- Use less-traditional methods of gathering data, such as flow charts, histograms, scattergrams, and force-field analyses.

Effective instructional leaders devote a great deal of time to number crunching. They have clear ideas of what constitutes success, and they use a variety of data sources to determine if their achievement goals have been reached. Dave Burton, a middle school principal, doesn't rely on just one measure. He's constantly assessing teaching and learning, especially during his frequent forays into the hallways, cafeteria, and team planning periods. He says, "I look at the analysis of standardized test scores, review student grades quarterly, make frequent classroom observations, and talk with teachers and students almost daily."

> An emphasis on results is central to school improvement.
>
> (Schmoker, 1999, p. 3)

Focus on fundamentals:
curriculum, instruction,
assessment, [and] professional
culture.

(Fullan, 1997, p. 28)

School improvement is like a race—with one major difference. The race is never really over. There is rarely a clear finish where we can declare a winner. Schools are in a constant state of flux. There *are* brief moments where we can celebrate regarding marvelous milestones, and then the race begins anew with an entirely new group of runners. Teachers resign and new ones are hired. New students enroll and others transfer to different schools. New textbooks are adopted. Instructional leaders must continually monitor and adjust. New staff members and parents must be informed and brought on board. The temptation to limit the inner circle of leadership to experienced and supportive staff members and parents is a strong one. Don't overlook, however, the need for involving everyone at key points along the way. Holcomb (1999) recommends involving all staff members whenever the following activities are taking place:

ESTABLISHING, IMPLEMENTING, AND ACHIEVING ACADEMIC STANDARDS IN A HIGH SCHOOL: JAMES EDWARDS, PRINCIPAL; LAURA GALIDO, GARY MAYEDA, YVONNE PECK, AND PHYLLIS THROCKMORTON, ASSISTANT PRINCIPALS

Oxnard High School, Oxnard, California

The energies of the entire administrative team at Oxnard High School are focused on instructional improvement and the achievement of academic standards. Established in 1901, Oxnard High School has a rich and colorful history. It currently serves over 3,000 culturally and economically diverse students (Latino, 62 percent; Anglo, 21 percent; African American, 6 percent; Asian, 4 percent; Filipino, 4 percent; Native American, 2 percent; and Pacific Islander, 1 percent). Under Proposition 98, schools in California are required to prepare an annual School Accountability Report Card.

(continued)

- Developing and affirming the school's mission
- Identifying significant, meaningful data to be compiled for the school portfolio
- Interpreting the data, requesting more data, and identifying areas of concern
- Focusing areas of concern on a few priorities and developing goals
- Participating in study groups to further analyze improvement concerns, select indicators of improvement, and recommend validated strategies
- Affirming the completed school improvement plan
- Participating in staff development to learn the use of new strategies and assessments
- Discussing evidence of progress with implementation and goal attainment. (pp. 90-91)

I would recommend keeping a representative sampling of your parent community involved with this process as well.

HOW CAN YOU USE THE INSTRUCTIONAL LEADERSHIP CHECKLIST TO ASSESS STEP ONE?

Step One: Establish, Implement, and Achieve Academic Standards

There are four indicators that describe step one in more detail. Each indicator is followed by three sections: (a) a *comment* that defines the specific focus of the indicator; (b) a *scale of descriptors* that gives a continuum of behaviors (1 to 5) from least effective to most effective; and (c) *key points in the descriptors* that give succinct explanations of each of the five items in the scale. For each indicator, select the number from 1 to 5 that most accurately describes your own behavior on a day-to-day basis.

Indicator 1.1

Incorporates the designated state and district standards into the development and implementation of the local school's instructional programs.

Comment

The main focus of Indicator 1.1 is the support the principal gives to mandated state and district standards while developing and implementing an instructional program that also meets the needs of the individual students, classrooms, and the school as a whole.

Scale of Descriptors

1. Principal does not support the use of state and district standards as the basis for the instructional program.

2. Principal pays lip service to the use of state and district standards as the basis

---

Oxnard High School
(continued)

Student achievement and demonstrated progress toward meeting academic standards are reported in terms of an Academic Performance Index (API). Administrators and teachers at Oxnard are currently engaged in a school improvement initiative that focuses on improvement in two major areas in an effort to increase their API.

Teachers and administrators have jointly identified functional and textual reading, as well as language mechanics, as very low areas of achievement by disaggregating the data from the SAT 9 test. All of the teachers have received an inservice on how to use both the standardized test data and formative classroom assessments to identify areas of weakness in their students and, in turn, tailor their lesson plans to target those areas. A group of freshmen and sophomore students who are reading well below grade level have been targeted to receive a period of direct instruction in reading at their specific instructional level in addition to their regular English class. The second period of the school day has been lengthened by 8 minutes, and all teachers (regardless of their subject matter assignment) are teaching a daily oral-language lesson to the students. The current emphasis on language development and reading proficiencies, with the goal of improving student achievement, has been communicated to students and parents. The assistant principals facilitate implementation by making informal, random, drop-in visits to classrooms to ensure that lessons are being taught.

MUST-READ BOOKS TO ASSIST YOU IN IMPLEMENTING STEP ONE

F. English. (1992). *Deciding What to Teach and Test: Developing, Aligning, and Auditing the Curriculum.* Thousand Oaks, CA: Corwin.

E. Holcomb. (1999). *Getting Excited About Data: How to Combine People, Passion, and Proof.* Thousand Oaks, CA: Corwin.

K. Leithwood, R. Aitken, & D. Jantzi. (2001). *Making Schools Smarter: A System for Monitoring School and District Progress.* Thousand Oaks, CA: Corwin.

E. K. McEwan. (1998). *The Principal's Guide to Raising Reading Achievement.* Thousand Oaks, CA: Corwin Press. (For elementary instructional leaders.)

E. K. McEwan. (2000). *The Principal's Guide to Raising Mathematics Achievement.* Thousand Oaks, CA: Corwin. (For elementary, middle, and high school instructional leaders.)

E. K. McEwan. (2001). *Raising Reading Achievement in Middle and High Schools: Five Simple-to-Follow Strategies.* Thousand Oaks, CA: Corwin.

M. Schmoker. (1999). *Results: The Key to Continuous Improvement.* Alexandria, VA: Association for Curriculum and Supervision Development.

for the school's instructional program but permits teachers to exercise personal judgments regarding their ultimate inclusion.

3. Principal believes that state and district standards should be used as the basis for the school's instructional program and communicates these expectations to teachers.

4. Principal believes that state and district standards should be the basis for the school's instructional program, communicates these expectations to teachers, and works with them in the development of instructional programs that do this effectively.

5. Principal believes that state and district standards should be the basis for the school's instructional program, communicates these expectations to teachers, works with them in the development of instructional programs that do this effectively, and monitors classroom activities and instruction to ensure such inclusion.

Key Points in Descriptors

1. No incorporation of state or district standards into program

2. Belief in importance but permissive in supervision

3. Belief in importance with expectations communicated

4. Belief in importance, expectations communicated, and assistance provided

5. Belief in importance, expectations communicated, assistance provided, and implementation monitored

Indicator 1.2

Ensures that schoolwide and individual classroom instructional activities are consistent with state, district, and school standards and are articulated and coordinated with one another.

Comment

The main focus of Indicator 1.2 is the match between the highest level of academic standards—whether those be state, school, or district—and what is happening in individual classrooms and the school as a whole; and what the principal is doing to ensure that consistency exists in each classroom in the building. The existence of clear standards is a *given* in this indicator.

Scale of Descriptors

1.   Although state, district, and school standards do exist, many activi-ties act as deterrents or impediments to the achievement of those standards.

2.   Although state, district, and school standards do exist, instructional practices in the school as a whole (majority of classrooms) do not appear to support the achievement of those standards.

3.   Although instructional practices in the school as a whole appear to support the state, district, and school standards, there are many individual classrooms in which instructional activities and outcomes do not support the stated standards.

4.   Instructional activities and student achievement in *most* classrooms and the school as a whole support the stated standards.

5.   Instructional activities in *all* classrooms and the school as a whole support the state, district, and school academic standards.

Key Points in Descriptors

1. Level 1 implies that the principal is unwilling to address a lack of consistency in *many* classrooms (more than half) or in the school as a whole.

2. Level 2 implies that the principal expresses a verbal willingness to address lack of consistency but fails to follow through with actions to ensure consistency.

3. Level 3 implies that the principal is willing to address a lack of consistency between standards and instruction but is marginally effective in doing so.

4. Level 4 implies that the principal is willing to ensure consistency between standards and instruction and is usually very effective in doing so.

5. Level 5 implies that the principal is highly effective in ensuring that instructional activities and outcomes match standards.

Indicator 1.3

Uses multiple sources of data, both qualitative and quantitative, to evaluate progress and plan for continuous improvement.

Comment

The main focus of Indicator 1.3 is the use of multiple assessments and sources of data by the principal and, in turn, the teachers to evaluate and, if necessary, make subsequent adjustments in instruction or curriculum to ensure that state, district, and school academic standards are being achieved.

Scale of Descriptors

1. No internal schoolwide program of assessment or data collection exists.

2. Although a district or schoolwide standardized testing program exists, the results are merely disseminated to teachers and parents; the principal does not use the information to help teachers evaluate and improve the instructional program.

3. Standardized test information is the sole indicator used by the principal for program evaluation. Review of the information is not systematic or specific, and teachers rarely review the results beyond the initial report.

4. Results of multiple-assessment methods—such as ongoing curriculum-based assessments, criterion-referenced tests, standardized tests, and performance or portfolio assessments—are systematically used and reviewed by the principal along with teachers.

5. Results of multiple-assessment methods are systematically used to evaluate program objectives. A schoolwide database that contains longitudinal assessment data for each student, classroom teacher, and grade level, as well as for the whole school, is regularly used by the principal and teachers to make instructional and program modifications for the school, individual classrooms or grade levels, and individual students, and to set meaningful and measurable goals for subsequent school improvement.

Key Points in Descriptors

1. No testing program

2. Standardized testing program with little use of results by either principal or teachers

3. Standardized testing program with some use of results by principal and little use of results by teachers

4. Well-rounded evaluation program with some use of results by both principal and teachers

5. Well-rounded evaluation program with effective use of results by both principal and teachers to modify and improve program

Indicator 1.4

Instructional leadership efforts on the part of the principal result in meaningful and measurable achievement gains.

Comment

The main focus of Indicator 1.4 is the achievement of measurable gains on a state assessment or local standardized test as a result of sustained instructional leadership and improvement efforts led by the principal.

Scale of Descriptors

1. The principal believes instructional leadership is no different from management and is unwilling to devote time and resources to improvement efforts toward raising achievement.

2. The principal pays lip service to the concept of instructional leadership, the development of goals, and school improvement activities but does nothing to provide resources or support to teachers.

3. The principal believes that instructional leadership is important, engages in some goal-setting and school improvement activities, but is unable to provide the support and resources that are necessary to bring about change.

4. The principal believes that instructional leadership is essential, engages in many meaningful goal-setting and school improvement activities, provides some support and resources that have resulted in some measurable achievement gains, but is unable to hold all teachers accountable and sustain improvement or realize meaningful gains for more than 1 year.

5. The principal believes that instructional leadership is key, engages in meaningful goal-setting and school improvement activities, provides strong support and ample resources, and has led the staff to meaningful achievement gains that have been sustained over time.

Key Points in Descriptors

1. No instructional leadership toward school improvement.

2. Minimal effort given to instructional leadership, goal setting, and school improvement activities. No resources or support provided to teachers. No gains.

3. Some instructional leadership. Some goal-setting and school improvement activities. Limited resources and support. No gains.

4. Excellent instructional leadership. Meaningful goal-setting and school improvement activities. Provision of resources and support. Limited accountability for all teachers. Minimal gains.

5. Strong instructional leadership. Meaningful goal-setting and school improvement activities. Provision of resources and support. Consistent accountability. Sustainable gains.

Step Two: Be an Instructional Resource for Your Staff

In the first edition of this book, step two read as follows: *be there for your staff*. While there was no doubt about the meaning of that statement to someone who read the associated chapter thoroughly, there were some occasions when the list of steps was published without the accompanying indicators and comments, giving rise to confusion. I have known principals who were there for their staff members in the sense that their offices were always open for friendly conversation, marital counseling, a bit of gossip, a cup of coffee, or just a good, old-fashioned gripe session. However, instruction, learning, or student achievement were never discussed. The principal and teacher were just colleagues doing what colleagues often do with each other. Of course, there will always be occasions when a principal offers support and encouragement to someone who is going through a difficult personal problem or family crisis, but the focus of step two is purely instructional, and any administrative support that is offered is solely for the purpose of enhancing the learning community, either in that teacher's classroom or in the school as a whole.

HOW CAN YOU WORK WITH TEACHERS?

Effective instructional leaders function as unique amalgams of ombudspersons, reference librarians, and genies-in-a-bottle who are constantly helping faculty to find the solutions they need to solve frustrating and difficult instructional problems. They regularly brainstorm with

> Most principals spend relatively little time in classrooms and even less time analyzing instruction with teachers. They may arrange time for teachers' meetings and professional development, but they rarely provide intellectual leadership for growth in teaching skill.
>
> (Fink & Resnick, 2001, p. 598)

teachers and bounce ideas around in both structured meetings and brief encounters. They rarely say no to new ideas and encourage teachers to try alternative techniques without fear of failure. They consistently attempt to match teacher with teacher to share common problems or solutions and teacher with resources to get the job done. They help teachers reflect on their own teaching and empower them to reach out for personal solutions. They are active listeners who always have time to empathize with a teacher's concern. Their doors are generally open, and when they talk with teachers, they do things like clear their tables of other work, take notes, paraphrase, and give feedback. They are willing to share ownership of any teacher's problem and do not point fingers, assign blame, or become judgmental. They respond immediately to any call for help from any teacher.

> The leader must have an infectious optimism and the determination to persevere in the face of difficulties. . . . The final test of a leader is the feeling you have when you leave his presence after a conference. Have you a feeling of uplift and confidence?
>
> (Montgomery, 1961, pp. 13-14)

Instructional leaders are also resource providers who are adept at finding and allocating money, planning and developing programs, and motivating people (parents and community) to become involved with their schools. They are constantly on the lookout for opportunities. They are masters at working the crowd. They are prolific grantwriters. When they see a need, they find a way. They do not know the meaning of the word no. They build school-business partnerships, seek out community support, and champion the causes of their school to anyone who will listen. Instructional leaders also know the importance of fostering harmonious and productive relationships with superintendents, curriculum directors, and other staff resource people; all these individuals can help the instructional leaders offer more resources to their staff.

Effective instructional leaders do all these things and more by utilizing the four Cs—Collaboration, Collegiality, Cooperation, and Creative Problem Solving. Their calendars are filled with meetings that focus on the four Cs:

- Meeting: child-study team to brainstorm solutions to a learning problem

  Result: a plan to try a different instructional methodology in the area of reading

- Meeting: building leadership team to facilitate the development of building staff development goals

Result: the development of goals in the area of peer coaching and mentoring for the faculty

- Meeting: parents of a gifted student, the media specialist, the classroom teacher, and the student

Result: an independent research project that will involve field trips with the parents that support class work

- Meeting: the math department regarding the new state assessment

Result: math department chair to attend workshop and bring back materials and present workshop to math teachers

- Meeting: the fifth-grade team to discuss the new math program implementation

Result: decision to purchase more materials to help with concepts in fractions and hiring a math consultant to do a demonstration lesson in each teacher's classroom

- Meeting: one of the middle school teams that is planning an overnight field trip and wants to talk through some problems they are having

Result: problem solved with a clever bit of wordless advice (nodding, looking concerned) on the part of the principal.

Rarely do effective instructional leaders enter a meeting room with a preconceived idea about how a problem should be solved; yet in each case, through collaboration, cooperation, collegiality, and creative problem solving, the participants emerge feeling empowered and energized with an action plan.

> Coaching is face-to-face leadership that pulls together people with diverse backgrounds, talents, experiences and interests, encourages them to step up to responsibility and continued achievement, and treats them as full-scale partners and contributors.
>
> (Peters & Austin, 1985, p. 264)

PROVIDING RESOURCES TO HELP TEACHERS AND STUDENTS SUCCEED: KATHIE DOBBERTEEN, PRINCIPAL

La Mesa Dale Elementary School, La Mesa, California

Kathie Dobberteen's expectations for student achievement are extraordinarily high, as are her expectations for teachers. She has not, however, expected them to do more with less, as is often the case. She has worked tirelessly to facilitate teamwork, find funding for additional staff members, and provide staff development.

We have moved from several team-teaching situations where the majority of classrooms still operated independently to the current status where it is truly a whole-school approach to instruction. Grade levels align curriculum to the standards, plan instruction, and provide for individual student needs. As a school, we have moved from merely making lesson plans to analyzing instruction, setting goals and objectives for student learning, and then collecting data to ensure the desired learning has occurred. Individual teachers no longer enter their classrooms and close the door to the outside

(continued)

La Mesa Dale Elementary School (continued)

world. As teams, they meet and plan together; they no longer are responsible for just their particular students. Instead, as a grade level, they are responsible for the entire student body at that grade level.

Our program used to be defined by a teacher's favorite theme and instructional expertise. The program is now currently defined by the standards and appropriate instruction to ensure students meet those standards. Our staff now believes that every student can be taught our new, rigorous California State Standards, but we have to provide additional time and interventions to make sure this happens. Some examples of the practices that have changed include the structure of both our reading and math programs. We have organized our reading program so that it is much more balanced, and each year we have looked for ways to make improvements. We started by hiring additional reading specialists for first and second grade. The next year, we hired college student aides so that we could complete guided reading in 30-minute sessions for all students in each classroom. This meant that more time was available for other language arts activities, especially shared reading and writing. The following year, we began conducting guided process reading Monday through Friday (instead of Monday through Thursday) to provide 20 percent more guided-process reading instruction. We targeted vocabulary, higher-order thinking skills, and a writing connection to be included in this 30-minute period. (Dobberteen, 2001, p. 3)

HOW CAN YOU SHARE RESEARCH AND BEST PRACTICES?

Effective instructional leaders take personal responsibility for making sure that trustworthy research and proven practices are talked about frequently and demonstrated ably in their schools. They make it happen. But they don't do it all by themselves. Mary Ann Friend encourages teachers to share their talents:

> To take advantage of this often-neglected resource, I began to have a sharing time at each staff meeting. Last year, the sharing was voluntary. Several of the sharing teachers put together a presentation for a district inservice. This year, sharing is required.

Paul Zaander asks teachers who attend workshops to make presentations when they return. He also arranges with a local university to hold classes in his building, thereby ensuring a high degree of participation from his teachers. Andy Bertram encourages his teachers to pursue advanced degrees and even sorts the mail himself so he can make sure that the appropriate flyers and advertisements for staff development opportunities get into the right mailboxes.

Effective instructional leaders are eager learners. They read a variety of publications, attend all kinds of workshops, go to national conferences, present staff development programs to their teachers, and are constantly on the lookout for potential resources for their buildings. They keep a

file of speakers, articles, and ideas to pull out
when the right moment presents itself in a conversation with a teacher.

> If teachers talked more with each other about both education and students, the chances for productive exchange about the effects of their efforts on students would increase.
>
> (Powell, Farrar, & Cohen, 1985, p. 320)

Many instructional leaders conduct action
research in their own buildings with local col-
leges or foundations. Carol Auer and her faculty
have teamed up with the Ball Foundation of
Glen Ellyn, Illinois, to find out if student
achievement will be impacted by increased
parent-teacher contacts that take place in alternative settings like homes,
restaurants, or the workplace. Following are a variety of other ways
that effective instructional leaders introduce their teachers to learning
opportunities:

• Provide copies of pertinent articles in teachers' mailboxes. Don't
overdo this practice or your paper budget will explode. But do find ways
to weave research findings that you think may have relevance to your
teachers into your conversations and presentations. Staff members will
soon discover what's hot and what's not and begin reading on their own.
A word of caution: make it clear to your staff that you are simply expanding their views and encouraging them to think. When an idea or strategy
has the potential for schoolwide implementation, reassure teachers that
plenty of brainstorming, discussion, problem solving, and decision
making will take place before implementation.

• Ask a local university to place student teachers in your building.
Working with an enthusiastic young educator who has been recently
trained can often be a motivator for a veteran staff member.

• Act as a seed planter in your school. When you see an example of
outstanding teaching or a particularly creative lesson, ask the teacher's
permission to share the idea with someone else. Teachers who might be
reticent to brag about their own work are usually delighted when the principal does it for them.

• Encourage teachers to do term papers and other class projects for
their advanced-degree work on topics of interest and concern to the
faculty. Ask them to share. One of my teachers who was working on her
doctorate in curriculum and instruction researched the issue of homework and its effectiveness, when we were preparing our school homework
policy. Many universities offer field-based degree programs. Assist your
teachers in choosing their areas of study to maximize the impact on your
school.

All men by nature desire knowledge.

(Aristotle, 1993, p. 3)

• Plan a yearly overnight, a weekend retreat, or just a casual gathering at someone's home. These times away are perfect to talk about new ideas, brainstorm creatively, or develop goals for the coming year. Instructional leaders use these techniques and find them helpful to get everyone into a relaxed setting removed from the pressures and time crunches that characterize so many faculty gatherings.

• Purchase videotapes that emphasize topics, instructional strategies, and curriculum that you are highlighting. Organize a systematic circulation program so that everyone has a chance to view them. Schedule a round-table discussion at a faculty meeting.

• Encourage staff members to develop expertise in certain areas so they can function as specialists on your staff. Include topics on department meetings that encourage department chairpersons to share information and experiences.

• Encourage teachers who are willing to pilot programs or instructional strategies in their classrooms so they can share with others who may need more help and encouragement.

• Take advantage of every opportunity to share your values about teaching and learning—through what you write in evaluation instruments, through what you say in postobservation conferences, through how you interact in brief hallway encounters, and in what you choose to focus on in formal staff development presentations.

MUST-READ BOOKS TO ASSIST YOU IN IMPLEMENTING STEP TWO

Jo Blase & Joseph Blase. (1998). *How Really Good Principals Promote Teaching and Learning.* Thousand Oaks, CA: Corwin.

R. P. DuFour & R. Eaker. (1998). *Professional Learning Communities at Work: Best Practices for Enhancing Student Achievement.* Bloomington, IN: National Education Service.

E. K. McEwan. (2001). *Ten Traits of Highly Effective Teachers: How to Hire, Mentor, and Coach Successful Teachers.* Thousand Oaks, CA: Corwin.

HOW CAN YOU KEEP YOUR FINGER ON THE INSTRUCTIONAL PULSE?

This aspect of instructional leadership can best be described as the day-to-day, week-to-week informal assessment of how well the instructional program is meeting the needs of individual students. "Dip-stick" daily to make sure that everything is running smoothly in every classroom. Determine how well individual students and groups of students in each classroom are doing by examining curriculum-based assessments, quizzes, or writing assignments. Manage by walking around. Put your finger on the collective pulse of the school, and find out if the heart is still beating. Is everyone on track? Is everyone keeping the faith?

"How are things going in your classroom?" This key question must be asked of every teacher on a regular basis. It is asked, *not* to evaluate the teacher's performance but to ascertain what else you as the instructional leader could be doing to help that teacher. Focus not on the teacher but on the goals that have been established by that grade level, department, and team. Ask questions, not to interrogate or judge but to make sure that you are aware at any given time of where the hot spots in your building are. What classrooms need your presence? What teachers need the behavior management specialist for consultation? Who needs the services of an instructional aide? What additional resources are needed to accomplish the goals? Accompanying questions might also include:

- Do you have all the materials you need to get the job done?
- Are all the children in your class experiencing success?
- Do you have any serious behavior problems that concern you?
- Is there anything about this year that surprises you?
- What's your best success story so far?
- What has you most frustrated about your class(es) this year?
- How's the new math program (or any other new program or text-book) working? Any concerns?
- Is there anything I can do to help?

Some teachers, especially those individuals who are confident and resourceful, will share with you regularly about what is going on in their classrooms. They will delight in reporting their successes and enlisting your help with problems. But others, particularly if the school culture has not always supported openness and sharing, will be reticent to share problems with the principal. They may feel they are complaining or that their problems will be tallied up for a subsequent write-up on an evaluation. These attitudes will change as your staff comes to know, respect, and trust you as an instructional leader.

IS IT REALLY POSSIBLE TO KNOW WHAT IS GOING ON?

"The more knowledgeable you are about what is happening in the class-rooms, the more effective you can be." Instructional leaders like Paul Zaander push themselves to be out in classrooms. They call it being there for the teachers. Often their paperwork suffers, but instructional leaders frequently stay in the office after everyone has left the building to tackle

> A school should be, above all
> else, a community of learners.
> Principals learn. Teachers learn.
> Parents learn. Student teachers
> learn. Visitors learn. And to
> the degree that they learn,
> students also learn.
>
> (Barth, 1980, p. 71)

the paper piles that inevitably develop during each day. Frequent drop-ins of 10 to 15 minutes per classroom enable principals to cover at least five to seven classrooms per day. Some carry a clipboard to keep records of the drop-ins or notes of things to do when they return to the office (books to order, support staff to contact). The information and insights they acquire while wandering enable them to support teachers and to get to know students in different ways. Principals of large elementary schools, middle schools, or high schools have more classrooms to cover, but with the assistance of support personnel, the job can be done. "There is no substitute for getting into classrooms and seeing what is going on," says high school principal Alan Jones. "One postconference is worth a thousand memos on effective instruction."

Merry Gayle Wade refuses to let the administrivia of a building principalship get her down. "Fifty percent of my time is spent visiting classrooms and an additional 25 percent working with teachers to improve their teacher effectiveness skills." Carol Auer has classroom visitation as her number one priority as well. "There is always some other thing that needs attending to—in fact, 100 other things, but if observing is important to you, you find the time to spend in the classroom."

Instructional leaders do more than just walk through the classrooms. They read stories, act as instructional aides, and teach units of instruction as well. But no matter what they are doing, it is their visible presence that matters. Nancy Carbone feels, "It sends a signal to the entire staff that good instruction and the carrying out of curriculum goals are important."

> Leaders develop and maintain
> collaborative relationships formed
> during the development and
> adoption of the shared vision.
> They form teams, support team
> efforts, develop the skills groups
> and individuals need, and provide
> the necessary resource, both
> human and material, to fulfill the
> shared vision.
>
> (Mendez-Morse, 2001, p. 4)

Instructional leaders spend more time in the classrooms of teachers they perceive as weak or needing help. Harvey Alvy explains that "When you hire good folks, you need to have faith in them, but with marginal staff, you need to know everything that's going on." Although they may not visit every classroom every day, effective instructional leaders have a strong sense of what is happening in each classroom. Student and parent opinion help to shape these perceptions, and so do frequent conversations with staff about their beliefs and values with regard to teaching and learning. But nothing beats first-hand knowledge. "The only way to get to the heart of the matter is to be there. The classroom is the heart and soul of the school, and to keep a finger on the pulse, you must be in the classroom," says high school principal Gary Catalani.

HOW CAN YOU USE THE INSTRUCTIONAL LEADERSHIP CHECKLIST TO ASSESS STEP TWO?

Step Two: Be an Instructional Resource for Your Staff

There are three indicators that describe this step in more detail. Each indicator is followed by three sections: (a) a *comment* that defines the specific focus of the indicator; (b) a *scale of descriptors* that gives a continuum of behaviors (1 to 5) from least effective to most effective; and (c) *key points in the descriptors* that give succinct explanations of each of the five items in the scale. For each indicator, select the number from 1 to 5 that most accurately describes your own behavior on a day-to-day basis.

Indicator 2.1

Works with teachers to improve instructional programs in their classrooms consistent with student needs.

Comment

The main focus of Indicator 2.1 is the role of the principal as an instructional resource for teachers in solving specific instructional problems related to student learning. Quality and quantity of assistance are to be considered as well as frequency with which teachers call on the principal for assistance.

Scale of Descriptors

1.   Principal has no interaction with teachers regarding the instructional program in their classrooms. Principal has almost no understanding of instructional program. Teachers never ask for instructional assistance from the principal, preferring to deal with instructional matters independently.

2.   Principal rarely assists teachers with instructional concerns but will attempt to assist a teacher if a specific, well-defined request is made. Principal has very sketchy knowledge and understanding of the instructional program. Teachers make few requests for assistance.

3.   Principal works in a limited way with those few teachers who request help. Principal's knowledge of instructional strategies is basic, and outside resources are often needed to solve instructional problems.

4. Principal works with most teachers through coordination and delegation, showing a strong degree of expertise. Teachers frequently turn to the principal for assistance.

5. Principal works with all teachers on a continuing basis and is an important resource for instructional concerns. The principal frequently initiates interaction, and teachers regularly turn to the principal for help, which is given with a high level of expertise.

Key Points in Descriptors

1. No interaction, no expertise, no requests for assistance

2. Little interaction, limited expertise, few requests for assistance

3. Some interaction, basic expertise, some requests for assistance

4. Frequent interaction, strong expertise, frequent requests for assistance

5. Regular interaction, outstanding expertise, regular requests for assistance

Indicator 2.2

Facilitates instructional program development based on trustworthy research and proven instructional practices.

Comment

The main focus of Indicator 2.2 is the status of the principal as an active learner in the acquisition of current educational research and practice and how effectively this knowledge base is shared and translated into instructional programs.

Scale of Descriptors

1. Principal is unaware of current, trustworthy educational research and proven practices.

2. Principal may be aware of current, trustworthy educational research and proven practices but feels this body of knowledge has little bearing on the day-to-day functioning of the school.

3. Principal is aware of current, trustworthy educational research and proven practices and believes they should affect program develop-ment but is not currently attempting to translate this information into practice.

4. Principal is aware of current, trustworthy educational research and proven practices, believes they should affect program development, shares them actively with staff, and is currently attempting to translate this information into instructional program development.

5. Principal is aware of current, trustworthy educational research and proven practices, believes they should affect program development, shares them actively with staff, and has successfully developed or altered school programs to reflect this knowledge base.

Key Points in Descriptors

1. No awareness of or belief in the importance or use of current educational research

2. Some awareness of but no belief in importance or use of current educational research

3. Some awareness of and belief in importance of but no use of current educational research

4. Awareness of, belief in importance of, and some attempts to translate information into instructional program

5. Awareness of, belief in importance of, and successful implementation of school programs based on research

Indicator 2.3

Uses appropriate formative-assessment procedures and informal data-collection methods for evaluating the effectiveness of instructional programs in achieving state, district, and local standards.

Comment

The main focus of Indicator 2.3 is the combination of multiple methods of evaluation by the principal that are formative in nature and indicate the need for immediate adjustments in instructional strategies, groupings, time allocations, lesson design, and so on. Examples of formative-evaluation tools are teacher-made tests; curriculum-based assessments; samples of student work; mastery-skills checklists; criterion-referenced tests; end-of-unit tests; observations in classrooms; and conversations with teachers, parents, and students.

Scale of Descriptors

1. Principal does not receive any regular, formative-evaluation information from classroom teachers.

2. Principal receives some formative-evaluation information from some classroom teachers, but sharing of this information is voluntary.

3. Principal solicits some formative-evaluation information regularly from all classroom teachers.

4. Principal solicits some formative-evaluation information regularly from all classroom teachers and discusses this information with teachers.

5. Principal solicits comprehensive, formative-evaluation information regularly from all classroom teachers, discusses this information with teachers, and, together with teachers, plans for changes in day-to-day classroom practices to increase instructional effectiveness.

Key Points in Descriptors

1. No regular, formative-evaluation information

2. Some voluntary, formative-evaluation information

3. Formative-evaluation information solicited regularly

4. Formative-evaluation information solicited regularly and discussed

5. Formative-evaluation information solicited regularly, discussed, and instructional practices adjusted

Step Three: Create a School Culture and Climate Conducive to Learning

Culture is the way things are done in an organization, and climate is the way people feel about that culture. Culture is made up of the feelings, beliefs, and values of staff members, students, and teachers that evolve over time. Do teachers in the building feel empowered? Do they believe that all children can learn? Are problems typically solved through consensus and conflict resolution, or are they swept under the rug? Do people talk about the good stuff of education, or does the lounge talk focus on picayune complaints? Do parents feel valued and welcome at the school, or are they fearful of asking questions and confronting problems? Climate has to do with the way people feel about the culture. Do people enjoy spending time with each other? Is school a pleasant place to be? When you walk in the door, do you get a good feeling? The scientific meaning of the word *climate* relates to weather phenomena—clouds, sunshine, thunder, or tropical breezes off the ocean. Those of us who spend time in many different schools (e.g., itinerant teachers, consultants, or central office administrators) can give an on-the-spot weather report after only a few minutes in a school. In some buildings, one can feel the black storm clouds hanging overhead. In

> Culture is an expression that tries to capture the informal, implicit—often unconscious—side of business or any human organization. Although there are many definitions of the term, culture in everyday usage is typically described as "the way we do things around here."
>
> (Deal, 1985, p. 601)

A HIGH SCHOOL CULTURE: ALAN JONES, PRINCIPAL

Community High School, West Chicago, Illinois

The culture that Alan Jones has created in his high school is focused on learning for both students *and* adults:

Every high school possesses a culture—a distinct theme that one feels in the hallways and when talking with teachers. The distinct theme that runs through the hallways of Community High School, a very diverse high school in the far western suburbs of Chicago, is its focus on the classroom teacher. While other principals in the area spend time developing different types of schedules, a new mission statement, or the implementation of new programs, such as block scheduling or authentic assessment, I have allocated my time and resources to frequent observation in classrooms and coaching of teachers along with the professional development of teachers. Early in my administration, the board of education granted my request for monies to support memberships in professional organizations and attendance at professional organizations. In addition to supporting teacher travel and membership dues, the board also provided more release time for department chairpersons to supervise teachers. Both these board policies have affirmed our belief that what happens in the classroom on a daily basis is the most important dynamic in student learning. After the approval of those policies, I developed systems that would give department chairpersons

(continued)

others, no matter what the weather is on the outside, it is always sunny, cheerful, upbeat, and optimistic inside.

HOW CAN YOU ESTABLISH HIGH EXPECTATIONS FOR STUDENTS?

The goal of establishing high expectations is a worthy one, but how can it be translated into the day-to-day behavior of the principalship? Most of us believe we have high expectations, but what do they look like? If this phrase becomes the rationale for high failure rates, then we have not achieved our goal. Alan Jones explains:

To foster academic achievement, schools need to do more than simply set demanding standards for children. They need to structure academic experiences in a way that enhances the students' sense of academic efficacy. Good instruction helps students at all levels, regardless of teacher expectations.

Effective instructional leaders do the following things to communicate high expectations to their students:

- Establish inclusive classrooms that send the message that all students are valued and can learn
- Provide extended learning opportunities for students who need them
- Observe and reinforce high expectations in the classroom that ensure an academically demanding climate and an orderly, well-managed classroom

- Ensure effective instruction that makes it possible for all students to learn
- Send messages to students that are focused on the importance of learning as well as the availability of staff and resources to help them
- Establish policies on student progress relative to homework, grading, monitoring progress, remediation, reporting progress, and retention or promotion that are consistent and equitable

Inclusive Classrooms

The tracking of students of varying ability levels, or the segregation of students with special needs, sends messages to these students and their parents that they don't have what it takes to make it in the regular classroom. Over the years, educators have sent the message that they need different teachers, different rooms, different textbooks, and a different set of expectations to succeed.

Instructional leaders have a big job ahead of them. Fortunately, many communities and districts are beginning to address these inequities. The West Chicago, Illinois, schools are including all their students with special needs in the regular classrooms. There are no self-contained, special education classes; rather, facilitating teachers and teacher assistants provide support to teachers who have students with disabilities in their classrooms. Research clearly documents the insidious effects of long-term tracking on lower-achieving students and students with special needs. There are clear differences between upper and lower tracks in regard

Community High School
(continued)

time and procedures to coach teachers on a regular basis, as well as give them the encouragement and resources they needed to pursue topics and interests in their disciplines. Today, every department in our school has staff members who regularly present at conferences. Other teachers have authored textbooks and articles in professional journals, and many have become leaders in various in-house staff development efforts. Most importantly, the culture of our building is focused in the classroom.

AN ELEMENTARY SCHOOL CULTURE: KATHIE DOBBERTEEN, PRINCIPAL

La Mesa Dale Elementary School, La Mesa, California

"We will not allow the demographics of the neighborhood to determine the destiny of our children. We are willing to do whatever it takes to make sure that children will be literate." Kathie Dobberteen wrote these words in her California Distinguished School application (Dobberteen, 2000). They are not empty platitudes; Kathie has led her staff to creation of a culture where students are not permitted to fail. That's not, however, the way it has always been. The *before* culture at La Mesa Dale was very different.

Seven years ago, La Mesa Dale was a typical elementary school staffed by caring teachers who worked in a self-contained environment;

(continued)

La Mesa Dale Elementary School (continued)

they were committed to doing their best for students in their classrooms. Collegiality was not a priority, and although camaraderie existed, the staff worked independently to meet the challenges of educating their students, who came primarily from low-income homes. Reading, while an important aspect of the educational process, was not a focus. It was treated with a remedial flavor—putting Band-Aids on small groups of children who were experiencing difficulties. The staff at La Mesa Dale lacked a common vision and felt no sense of personal accountability for the achievement of their students. The school was ruled by the belief that the low-socioeconomic status of our students meant we would have correspondingly low achievement. Although we sensed that change was needed, we initially grasped at anything that was new.

First, we focused on multicultural education, hoping to build acceptance and tolerance among our culturally diverse population. Then, we emphasized conflict resolution to encourage respect, self-reliance, and student ownership of what took place at school. None of these programs had any impact on student achievement. (Dobberteen, 1999, 2000, 2001)

One variable that did have an impact on student achievement in Kathie's school was a total change in the culture. Now the teachers can say with one voice: *At La Mesa Dale, we are*

(continued)

to the following variables: content and quality of instruction, teacher-student and student-student relationships, the expectations of teachers for their students, the affective climate of classrooms, and other elements of the educational enterprise. "It appears that those students for whom the most nurturing learning would appear to be appropriate received the least" (Oakes, 1985, p. xi). Effective instructional leaders are beginning to change the way teachers look at tracking and grouping and, through careful planning with staff, are restructuring their classrooms.

A helpful checklist to assess tracking practices in your school is provided by Linn and Barquet (1992, pp. 16-17). Among the 40 questions they ask in areas such as staff expectations, student placement, and evaluation procedures are these:

- Has a survey of school culture or climate been undertaken to ensure that every student has the necessary personal and academic support to achieve the district's expectations?
- Are all students required to take more than 2 years of math and science at the high school level?
- Is the grouping of students for instructional purposes flexible, temporary, and intended to accelerate learning?
- Are critical thinking, expository writing, and oral presentations an integral part of all student programs?
- Is persistence taught, valued, and rewarded in all classes?
- Have students been followed after graduation to see what kinds of

jobs and education they have pursued—to determine the school's success in preparing students?

- Do staff members avoid using terms such as "bright students," "able learners," "college bound," "remedial," "lower track," and "LD" (learning disabled) to refer to specific groups of students?

- Are girls, students with low-socioeconomic status, minorities, physically disabled, and limited-English-speaking students represented in leadership roles such as student council and student government?

Extended Learning Opportunities

Instructional leaders who are committed to the belief that all children can achieve the established state, district, and school standards quickly realize the impossibility of attaining these goals if extended learning opportunities are not offered to the students who need them. The critical issue for educators should be not *when* a student learns something but *whether* a student learns something. Spady (1992) likens this commonsense principle to the Scout merit badge system, the apprenticeship program, or simply receiving a license to drive a car or fly a plane. Instructional leaders must find ways to break through the time barrier that keeps large numbers of students from achieving the standards that have been established.

La Mesa Dale Elementary School (continued)

absolutely determined not to let a single student slip through the cracks.[1]

Student achievement at La Mesa Dale is impressive. When the percentage of economically disadvantaged students scoring above the 50th percentile in reading at La Mesa Dale is compared to the rest of California, the percentages at La Mesa Dale are two to three times higher at every grade level than the state's averages. A student at La Mesa Dale Elementary School was overheard explaining how things worked at his school to some visitors: "Our teachers won't let us fail. That's why my mom sends us here!" (There is open enrollment in the La Mesa Dale District.) It is not enough just to have high expectations for students. The students must feel them on a daily basis.

If the conditions in which children live are such that the behavior of the principal does not make a difference in children's schooling, then we can blame our lack of performance on circumstances. . . . However, if it is true that what we do does have a profound effect on children's opportunities to succeed in our society, then the ethical and moral obligations prevail for us to create conditions in schools that reflect the best of what we know.

(Andrews, 1989, p. 4)

Teacher Expectations

Research over an extensive period of time has shown that teachers treat low-achieving students differently from high-achieving students. Teachers give more praise and approval to high-achieving than to low-achieving students. Children perceived as low achievers received fewer

When student demographics are framed as an equity issue, the educational goal created for schools and districts is to reduce their power to predict variation in student outcomes.

(Leithwood, Aitken, & Jantzi, 2001, p. 47)

EXTENDED LEARNING OPPORTUNITIES: KATHIE DOBBERTEEN, PRINCIPAL

La Mesa Dale Elementary School, La Mesa, California

The impressive achievement gains at La Mesa Dale that were described earlier in the chapter have resulted, in part, from the provision of multiple extended-learning opportunities.

At La Mesa Dale, we have totally changed the organizational structure of our school to reflect our belief that every child can master standards if given additional time to do so. These changes can be seen in the following ways:

• Students flexibly move between classrooms depending on their levels in reading, during guided-process reading.

• We provide additional instructional time through a daily enrichment tutorial period. During this part of the school day, students who need extra help have time to get it while other students have the benefit of enrichment.

• We provide additional time to master the standards through before-, during-, and after-school intervention programs in reading, math, technology, and English as a second language.

(continued)

reading turns, fewer opportunities to answer open or direct questions, fewer opportunities to make recitations, and they were less apt to call out answers (deGroat & Thompson, 1949). Children perceived by the teacher as high achievers received more praise and less criticism than children perceived as low achievers (Good & Brophy, 1971). Teachers often treat students from ethnic minorities differently as well. Mexican American students in one study experienced more interactions with the teacher than Anglos in only two areas—giving directions and criticizing. In all positive categories, the Anglos experienced more interactions (U.S. Commission on Civil Rights, 1973).

Researchers have cited 18 different *instructional* variables that differ between low-ability and high-ability students—for example, lower-ability students receive the least prepared teachers, are more likely to receive instruction from aides, and spend less time on interactive teaching and more with worksheets. They identify nine different *time* variables that differ between low-ability and high-ability students—for example, lower-ability students lose more instructional time in transitions, spend more class time devoted to homework, and spend more time with no work assignments. Finally, they cite 21 different variables related to *curriculum content*—for example, content for low-ability students is less academically oriented, material is covered at a slower pace, and fewer tests are given. They also cite three different variables of *success*—for example, low-ability students engage in more off-task behavior and have lower rates of success (Rosenbaum, 1980).

Instructional leaders have an obligation to carefully observe and monitor how teachers interact with both high-achieving and low-achieving students and to then provide training and assistance for teachers to help them change in the necessary areas. One powerful training program that has been used by many instructional leaders is Teacher Expectations and Student Achievement (Kerman, 1979). The program consists of five mini-units in each of three strands that emphasize the concept of equity of educational opportunity: response opportunities, feedback, and personal regard. The lessons take participants through 15 different ways in which teachers interact with students to raise expectations and thus achievement. Participants are encouraged to observe one another between each workshop session and collect data on their interactions with students. The units include information to assist teachers in learning how to

> **La Mesa Dale Elementary School** (continued)
>
> • Academic summer school (6 weeks) and a spring break intervention program (1 week) provide additional time for students to learn standards through focused instruction. (K. Dobberteen, 2001, p. 9)

> No amount of good feeling is adequate without that pedagogical dimension, without students actually knowing more and being able to do more at the end of a school year than they could at the beginning.
>
> (Kohl, 1998, p. 27)

- Equitably distribute among students the opportunity to respond
- Affirm or appropriately correct a student's response
- Position oneself and move around the classroom appropriately so that all students have an awareness of the teacher's presence
- Provide help to low achievers as frequently as to high achievers
- Praise the learning performance of lower achievers as frequently as that of other students
- Use courteous words as frequently with low achievers as with other students and as frequently with all students as with adults
- Give low achievers as much time to respond to a task or question as given to other students
- Tell low achievers as frequently as other students why their class work is acceptable or praiseworthy
- Give personal compliments to low achievers as frequently as to other students and express personal interest in the outside activities of low achievers as frequently as to those of other students
- Help all students to respond to questions by providing additional information to them
- Listen attentively to low achievers as well as to other students
- Touch low achievers in a friendly manner as frequently as high achievers

- Challenge the thinking abilities of low achievers as often as other students by requiring them to do more than simply recall information
- Convey to all students that their feelings are understood and accepted in a nonjudgmental manner
- Be cool and calm when stopping the misbehavior of low achievers, just as with high achievers.

Instructional Effectiveness

Holding high expectations for students without also providing top-notch instruction is tantamount to educational malpractice.

> There are those who argue that the successful teacher ought to be more concerned with the affective side of students rather than with the growth of cognitive skills. To a degree, this attitude may be correct, but to a larger degree, it is not. Bedside manner is often touted as being very important to a doctor's success. But how many patients choose the doctor with a more pleasant bedside manner over a doctor with a higher patient survival rate? (Scheidecker & Freeman, 1999, p. 35)

Highly effective teachers don't teach in just one way—they have a repertoire of instructional techniques, teaching behaviors, and essential skills on which to draw, depending on the needs of their students, the nature of the subject, and the complexity of the learning outcomes (Leithwood, Aitken, & Jantzi, 2001, pp. 85-86). The knowledge and research that presently exists to inform the practice of teaching is rich (McEwan, 2001). We do not know nearly all that we need to know, by any means. But we do know a great deal about what works. To perfect and polish a teaching repertoire takes time, experience, practice, quality staff development, and highly skilled clinical supervision from peers and administrators.

A Focus on Learning

Effective instructional leaders use a variety of techniques to keep students and teachers focused on the goal of learning for all. Sister Catherine Wingert uses community speakers throughout the year who relate the importance of high standards of work and act as role models for students. Other instructional leaders select school themes or mottoes. "Be the Best You Can Be" is the motto of James Simmons's school in Mountain

Home, Arkansas. He even has the motto printed on his business card. Stella Loeb-Munson and her staff in East Cleveland, Ohio, have borrowed Jesse Jackson's motto, "Conceive it, believe it, achieve it."

Although instructional leaders focus a great deal of attention on academic achievement, they also recognize that every student can't be at the top. Roger Moore and his staff in Lake City, Michigan, hold Personal Growth assemblies every month. In these assemblies, students are given awards for showing improvement. Parents are invited, and every student in the school receives at least one award each year. Diane Borgman and her staff in Soldotna, Alaska, have a "These Are Great Kids Board" in the hallway. Teachers place certificates on the board for accomplishments of students in their classrooms. Every child receives recognition before a new cycle begins.

> Classrooms are dynamic and complex societies that are rife with expectations: expectations that teachers have for students, and that students have for teachers and for each other. These expectations explain a good deal of what we see when we visit a classroom—both the good and the bad, the productive, and the wasteful. But the expectations themselves can't be seen. They hang in the air almost like an atmosphere; they exist only between people and comprise a part of their relationship.
>
> (Saphier & Gower, 1997, p. 47)

Policies That Promote Progress

Effective instructional leaders develop policies jointly with faculty members that address homework (Are assignments commensurate with grade levels and appropriate learning activities?); progress monitoring (Are parents notified immediately whenever students are falling behind or having a problem?); remediation (Are immediate steps taken when students are in academic trouble, or are they allowed to flounder for weeks?); progress reporting (Is there a system in place for reporting progress to parents?); and retention or promotion (Is there a policy that addresses the body of research showing the deleterious effects of retention on students?).

Shame on the teachers who do the following, as well their principals who overlook these discriminatory practices:

- Use varying grading scales
- Worship grade averages
- Use zeroes indiscriminately

> What makes a good school has very little to do with how rich or poor the students are or the type of curriculum that's taught. It has very little to do with special programs, expansive playing fields, huge endowments, snappy uniforms, celebrity alumni, or whether the school is wired to the Internet. What makes a good school, whether it's public or private, religious or nonreligious, charter or noncharter, is a feeling. A feeling shared by the entire staff that their particular school is special. The feeling that their school really belongs to them.
>
> (Manna, 1999)

- Follow the assign-test-grade-teach pattern of instruction
- Fail to maintain teaching-testing congruency
- Ambush students with pop quizzes
- Stack the deck against students
- Practice I-gotcha teaching
- Don't give students a second chance
- Penalize students for taking risks
- Establish individual criteria
- Fail to provide an appeals process

HOW CAN YOU MAKE SURE TIME IS BEING USED EFFECTIVELY?

Increasing academic learning time is a three-step process: (a) make sure that students are actually in class; (b) make sure that when students are in class, the time is being used for learning; and (c) make sure that students are achieving at a success rate of 90 to 95 percent.

How to Increase Student Attendance

We encounter organizational cultures all the time. When they are not our own, their most visible and unusual qualities seem striking. . . . When the cultures are our own, they often go unnoticed—until we try to implement a new strategy or program which is incompatible with their central norms and values. Then we observe, firsthand, the power of culture.

(Kotter & Heskett, 1992, p. 3)

- Make sure you read all the student attendance policies provided by the board of education. Then make sure they are clearly communicated to staff, students, and parents. Develop a schoolwide plan on attendance, including reporting and follow-up. Consistency on the part of all staff members is crucial for success.

- Use an automatic dialing system with prerecorded messages to contact homes about student absences.

- Send a letter to parents at the beginning of the school year stressing the importance of attendance and requesting that vacations not be taken during the school year.

- Support teachers in improving classroom management. Provide recognition for teachers who motivate students and require punctuality. Require teachers to check attendance promptly every day. Encourage teachers to greet students personally every day. Refer habitual attendance problems to counselors or truancy programs.

- Be consistent in enforcing rules on attendance and tardiness. Require parental excuses for returning students with medical excuses required for extended absences. Hold personal conferences with students after extended absences. Encourage attendance competitions between classrooms. Don't suspend students from school for truancy or tardiness. (McEwan, 1998)

How to Increase Allocated Learning Time

Getting students to school is only part of the time-on-task goal. Helping teachers focus on using that time efficiently and effectively is the second assignment for the instructional leader. The link between students being on task in the classroom and their academic achievement has been clearly established (Bloom, 1980; Rosenshine & Berliner, 1980; Stallings, 1980). Strong instructional leaders are constantly observing and taking note of the way all teachers use their time—not to play gotcha when staff members fail to measure up to expectations but to praise and reinforce the wise use of time. Excellent instructional leaders pay special attention to the behaviors that characterize effective teachers and are tirelessly working to increase the likelihood that all the teachers in the building will fill the bill. They use verbal praise, short notes of commendation, and formal evaluation procedures to constantly remind teachers of the importance of the following behaviors that characterize effective teachers:

- Spend at least half of their class time on interactive types of activities such as explaining new material, discussing and reviewing in small groups, hands-on activities, and project work
- Spend about one third of class time on actively monitoring silent reading, written work, and lab work
- Are rarely sitting at their desks waiting for students to come to them. They move about the classroom on the lookout for students who need help, particularly those students who have been targeted as needing help by the student support team
- Spend less than 15 percent of class time on classroom management and organization: passing paper, explaining activities, arranging desks, moving from one lesson to another, taking attendance, making announcements, and so on
- Have a list of behavior expectations that are clear, posted in view, and consistently reinforced
- Spend very little time in class socializing with students, visitors, or aides

- Plan daily activities in advance and make them clear to students by writing the day's schedule on the board
- Plan a variety of academic activities using differing modalities during one class period
- State the objectives and purpose of the lesson
- Give immediate feedback
- Focus most instruction on the whole class or small groups, rather than individuals
- Distribute opportunities for verbal response equally among students
- Praise student success and effort
- Give students who answer incorrectly another chance to get it right by rephrasing the question or giving hints
- Provide an overview or review before presentation of new material and a summary and explanation at the end. (Stallings, 1989)

How to Increase the Rate of Success for Students

> A positive school climate is perhaps the single most important expression of educational leadership.
>
> (S. Thomson, cited in Kelly, 1980)

Instructional leaders encourage programs and activities that motivate students, make learning meaningful, and involve students in all aspects of school life. These activities are as varied as the individual schools. Meaningful instruction is the most important component of any program or activity, however. In Mary Ann Friend's school, teachers believe that students learn best in an atmosphere that treats learning as an exciting, dynamic activity. Many instructional leaders provide extended opportunities for students who need more time to learn. At McPherson Middle School, Merry Gayle Wade has study labs, math labs, and an after-school tutorial center. Teachers provide study times before and after school for students who need it. Students are encouraged to retake tests if they fail them the first time. Wade and her staff place the importance on achievement of standards, not on *when* that achievement takes place. Lynn Sprick, a high school principal in Quincy, Illinois, provides support programs for students who need lots of follow-through and TLC, and an extended day for those needing a place to study, complete with resources and books. At Thornwood High School in West Chicago, Illinois, Gary Catalani and his staff provide a 40-minute communication period at the end of each day for tutoring.

Strong instructional leaders borrow ideas from others and adapt them to their own schools. They gather teachers, parents, and students together to brainstorm. Wherever and whenever there is a learning challenge, instructional leaders can find a way to overcome the hurdle.

DOES YOUR SCHOOLWIDE BEHAVIOR PLAN FACILITATE LEARNING?

A safe and orderly school climate is a lot like good plumbing. When it's working, no one pays much attention to it. People just go about the important business of living and working and learning. When it's broken (either the plumbing or student behavior), however, all meaningful activities cease until the problem is fixed. The existence of a safe and orderly climate appears on almost everyone's short list of what constitutes an effective school. The instructional

> The ambience of each school differs. These differences appear to have more to do with the quality of life and indeed the quality of education in schools than do the explicit curriculum and the methods of teaching.
>
> (J. Goodlad cited in Raywid, Tesconie, & Warren, 1985, p. 14)

leaders I interviewed believe that no student has the right to interfere with the learning of another student. They unequivocally state they will not deny the opportunity for others to learn at the expense of an undisciplined child. They are adamant about the importance of an environment that is safe and orderly so that learning can take place. They believe that school must be a safe haven for learning—safe from ridicule for having a wrong answer or not knowing. They recognize the importance of consistent schoolwide behavioral expectations. They also know that there is no *one* consequence or plan that works for all students and that sometimes consequences and plans need to be negotiated for individual students or problems. They focus on solving discipline problems in a way that is not punitive yet gets the situation under control while, at the same time, opening the student's mind to the option of beginning to work in class. They are in frequent contact with parents, have teams in their building to solve problems when they arise, and often counsel with students individually. They are constantly recognizing students for appropriate behavior and avoid problems before they happen by instituting programs that pair students and staff members in mentoring or significant-other relationships. Instructional leaders have outstanding student morale and behavior in their schools and firmly believe there is no problem for which a solution does not lie just around the corner.

Lasley and Wayson (1982) have summarized these qualities, but the comments in italics are mine:

- All faculty members and students are involved in problem solving. *Excluding anyone from the information and decision-making loop is bound to result in a pocket of resistance that can undermine any disciplinary structure.*

- The school is viewed as a place to experience success. *Mutual respect is the key to appropriate student behavior. If teachers and students continually play gotcha with each other, the system will break down.*

• Problem solving focuses on causes rather than symptoms. *What are the underlying causes that might be contributing to poor behavior— overcrowding, student frustration, punitive consequences, academic difficulties, ineffective instruction? Hopefully, your school uses a functional behavior analysis with students whose behavior is a problem just looking for a solution. (McEwan & Damer, 2000)*

• Emphasis is on positive behaviors and preventative measures.

• The principal is a strong leader. *There is no individual that impacts the school atmosphere as much as the school principal. Everyone looks to principals for direction, and they must provide it in ways both tough and tender.*

MUST-READ BOOKS TO ASSIST YOU IN IMPLEMENTING STEP THREE

R. L. Curwin & A. M. Mendler. (1999). *Discipline with Dignity.* Alexandria, VA: Association for Supervision and Curriculum Development.

T. E. Deal & K. D. Peterson. (1998). *Shaping School Culture: The Heart of Leadership.* San Francisco: Jossey-Bass.

R. DiGiulio. (2000). *Positive Classroom Management.* Thousand Oaks, CA: Corwin.

E. K. McEwan & M. Damer. (2000). *Managing Unmanageable Students: Practical Tips for Administrators.* Thousand Oaks, CA: Corwin.

HOW CAN YOU ALTER THE CULTURE AND CLIMATE OF YOUR SCHOOL?

Creating a school culture and climate that are conducive to learning is a challenging task for even the most effective instructional leader. But Deal (1985) has some suggestions that might prove helpful.

First, he advises exploring and documenting a school's history. This exercise can be particularly helpful for the new principal who needs to know what values have evolved from the common experiences previously shared by staff, parents, and students. Deal then suggests that heroes and heroines be anointed and celebrated:

At Lincoln Elementary School in West Chicago, Illinois, I noted that teachers often felt unappreciated, particularly those with many years of service. So, when the first retirement rolled around during my tenure, we established a tradition of celebrating the retirements of teachers and staff members with a schoolwide assembly. Skits were performed, students gave testimonials, family members and former staff members were invited, and a reception complete with receiving line was held. A special plaque in the hallway contained the names and dates of service for all retired staff members. We honored the custodian with the same kind of celebration as the kindergarten teacher. I wanted students to see the value and learn to appreciate all kinds of work. Students and staff were able to see the tangible rewards of a job well done. To celebrate our school's 70th anniversary, we invited all the teachers still living who had ever retired from their teaching careers in our school. They shared anecdotes about their experiences and participated in the receiving line also. Each year, we continued to anoint and celebrate heroes and heroines. This celebration remained a part of the culture of Lincoln School until it was closed in 1993.

Another way of developing a culture that supports learning is by reviewing the rituals. According to Deal, "living and meaningful rituals convey culture values and beliefs" (p. 616).

A ritual that characterized the opening of school each year for me as a building principal was the gathering on the playground of teachers, parents, and students on the first day. All the teachers carried large signs mounted on sticks. On the signs were written their names, grade level, and some suitable decorations. Students and parents consulted the class lists posted on the school doors and then found the teacher. All teachers greeted their students personally, checking them off the list and warmly welcoming them to school. In my role as principal, I wandered about the playground greeting parents, old and new, empathizing with those for whom the summer had seemed much too long as well as with those who were reluctant to say good-bye to their children. After the bell rang and each class moved into the building, small groups of parents continued to talk. I circulated to each group, reestablishing friendships and welcoming new faces. In the 8 years we went through this opening-day ritual, it never once rained. I had many contingency plans in my file, but fortunately, our ritual went unchanged.

Ceremonies are another strategy for building school culture. Pep rallies, assemblies, sports contests, and graduation exercises are all ceremonies that can build school spirit. I was privileged to attend such a ceremony in Joe Porto's school in Highland Park, Illinois. The pep assembly celebrated the essence of the school. Students were dressed in red and white, and each class had made up a cheer to show their pride in the school. From kindergarten to fifth grade, the cheers progressed in sophistication and complexity. They highlighted teachers, students, learning, and community. It was a remarkable event.

Remarkable in a different way was the pep assembly at a local high school that had won the state football championship. It provided a memorable ceremony for all the participants. Wearing new uniforms and carrying a new school name, the result of relocation to a larger facility, the team still retained their school mascot, a tiger. The tiger was the proud symbol of the past. As the principal, instructional leader Chuck Baker donned the tiger costume: some might call it silly. But Chuck recognized and used that ceremony and symbolism to create yet another story for the school's rich history and tradition.

Storytelling is yet another way to build or revitalize a school culture. Tales of championship teams and remarkable performances can motivate both students and teachers to become part of a winning team. Teachers and principals can relive success stories with children:

> Remember how we taught Vicki to read in third grade when everyone had given up on her? This year she's the captain of the Battle of the Books team. And remember the time the principal ran around the school in her bathing suit to spur us on to read more books? And who can forget when the custodian danced the polka with the principal at his retirement party?

At Phyllis O'Connell's school, the stories that are retold relate to the Fudd Award. To be eligible for posting on the Fudd Wall of Fame (after the wacky cartoon character Elmer Fudd) in the faculty lounge, a staff member must do something silly—like the individual who drove through the car wash with her windows down because she was so preoccupied with a school problem. It's a dubious honor to get a Fudd, but there is a camaraderie amongst the award winners that makes new staff members almost wish to be a part of this spacey crew.[2]

A final way to build culture is to encourage what Deal (1987) calls the network of priests or priestesses, gossips, storytellers, and other cultural players that keep the culture alive and intact:

> Old practices and other losses need to be buried and commemorated. Meaningless practices and symbols need to be analyzed and revitalized. Emerging visions, dreams, and hopes need to be articulated and celebrated. These are the core tasks that will occupy educational leaders for several years to come. (p. 14)

Another model proposes 12 norms of school culture that must be attended to in order for school improvement activities to have any effect. They are collegiality; experimentation; high expectations; trust and confidence; tangible supports; reaching out to the knowledge base; appreciation and recognition; caring, celebration, and humor; involvement in decision making; protection of what's important; traditions; and honest, open communication (Saphier & King, 1985). Linda Murphy, former principal and now superintendent, developed a brief questionnaire to be used by her faculty members to facilitate assessment and discussion of each of the norms (McEwan, 1997, p. 28):

> Shared values define the fundamental character of their organization, the attitude that distinguishes it from all others. In this way, they create a sense of identity for those in the organization, making employees feel special.
>
> (Deal & Kennedy, 1982, p. 23)

- What practices or conditions in my school currently strengthen this norm?
- What practices or conditions in my school currently weaken this norm?
- What is my vision of what this norm could be at its best?
- What ideas do I have to improve this norm?
- What would I be willing to do to improve this norm?

HOW CAN YOU USE THE INSTRUCTIONAL LEADERSHIP CHECKLIST TO ASSESS STEP THREE?

Step Three: Create a School Culture and Climate Conducive to Learning

There are three indicators that describe this step in more detail. Each indicator is followed by three sections: (a) a *comment* that defines the specific focus of the indicator; (b) a *scale of descriptors* that gives a continuum of behaviors (1 to 5) from least effective to most effective; and (c) *key points in the descriptors* that give succinct explanations of each of the five items in the scale. For each indicator, select the number from 1 to 5 that most accurately describes your own behavior on a day-to-day basis.

Indicator 3.1

Establishes high expectations for student achievement that are directly communicated to students, teachers, and parents.

Comment

The main focus of Indicator 3.1 concerns the philosophical assumptions the individual makes about the ability of all students to learn, the need for both equity and excellence in the educational program, and the ability to communicate these beliefs to students, teachers, and parents.

Scale of Descriptors

1. Principal believes that nonalterable variables, such as home background, socioeconomic status, and ability level, are the prime determinants of student achievement, and the school cannot overcome these factors.

2. Principal believes that the nonalterable variables cited above significantly affect student achievement and the school has a limited impact on student achievement.

3. Principal believes that although the nonalterable variables cited above may influence student achievement, teachers are responsible for all students mastering basic skills and prescribed learner outcomes according to individual levels of expectancy. The principal occasionally communicates these expectations in an informal way to teachers, parents, and students via written and spoken communications or specific activities.

4. Principal believes that although the nonalterable variables cited above may influence student achievement, teachers are responsible for all students mastering certain basic skills at their grade level and frequently communicates these expectations to teachers, parents, and students in a formal, organized manner. Expectations for student achievement may be communicated through written statements of objectives in basic skills or a written statement of purpose and mission for the school that guides the instructional program.

5. Principal believes that together the home and school can have a profound influence on student achievement. Teachers are held responsible not only for all students mastering certain basic skills at their grade level but also for the stimulation, enrichment, and acceleration of the student who is able to learn more quickly and the provision of extended learning opportunities for students who may need more time for mastery. Expectations for student achievement are developed jointly among parent, student, and teacher and are communicated not only through written statements of learner outcomes in core curriculum areas but also in enriched and accelerated programs, achievement awards, and opportunities for creative expression.

Key Points in Descriptors

1. No impact by school on students. No communication of achievement expectations to teachers, parents, or students.

2. Limited impact by school on students. No communication of achievement expectations to teachers, parents, or students.

3. All students should master basic learner outcomes. Limited communication of achievement expectations to teachers, parents, and students.

4. All students should master basic learner outcomes. Formal communication of achievement expectations to teachers, parents, and students.

5. All students master basic learner outcomes with many students exceeding the minimal competencies, participating in an enriched or accelerated course, and receiving academic awards. Joint development of achievement expectations by teachers, parents, and students.

Indicator 3.2

Establishes clear standards, communicates expectations for the use of time allocated to instruction, and monitors the effective use of classroom time.

Comment

The main focus of Indicator 3.2 is the existence of written guidelines for use of classroom time, the existence of a weekly program schedule for each classroom teacher, the regular monitoring of lesson plans, and the schoolwide schedule and its impact on instructional time.

Scale of Descriptors

1. Teachers are totally unsupervised in the planning of their daily schedule. No written guidelines exist for the use of classroom time. There are frequent interruptions that significantly interfere with instruction.

2. State, district, or school guidelines for the use of classroom time exist, but the principal does not monitor their implementation in the classroom. There are many interruptions to instructional time that could be avoided.

3. State, district, or school guidelines for the use of classroom time exist, and the principal monitors their implementation in the classroom by requiring teachers to post a copy of their weekly schedule and by occasionally reviewing lesson plans. There are some, but not frequent, interruptions.

4. State, district, or school guidelines for the use of classroom time exist; the principal monitors their implementation by requiring teachers to post a weekly program schedule and by regularly reviewing lesson plans. Basic skill instructional time is occasionally interrupted with advance notice. Whenever possible, interruptions are planned during noninstructional time.

5. State, district, or school guidelines for the use of classroom time exist, and the principal monitors regularly their implementation through the review of classroom or grade-level lesson plans and regular classroom visitations. Classroom instructional time is rarely interrupted, and the principal plans with teachers in the coordination of schoolwide schedules to minimize the effect of pullout programs, assemblies, and other special events.

Key Points in Descriptors

1. No guidelines

2. Guidelines, no monitoring, frequent interruptions

3. Guidelines, limited monitoring, limited interruptions

4. Guidelines, frequent monitoring, few interruptions

5. Guidelines, frequent monitoring, coordinated school schedule to minimize interruptions

Indicator 3.3

With teachers and students (as appropriate), establishes, implements, and evaluates procedures and codes for handling and correcting behavior problems.

Comment

The main focus in Indicator 3.3 is the existence of a behavior plan for each classroom and for the building as a whole, and the participation of the principal in the implementation of this plan. The focus of the plan is on responsible, caring behavior by all students and teachers based on mutual respect and common goals. Positive as well as negative reinforcers are included in the plan.

Scale of Descriptors

1. All classroom teachers have their own method of handling behavior problems without support or assistance from the principal, and there is no schoolwide behavior plan or comprehensive set of school rules.

2. All classroom teachers have their own methods of handling behavior, and no schoolwide behavior plan or set of school rules exists. The principal is available for assistance with severe behavior problems and handles them on an individual basis with little uniformity or consistency.

3. Each classroom teacher files a behavior plan with the principal, and rules for behavior in common areas of the building are available. The principal is generally supportive and provides assistance with behavior problems.

4. Each classroom teacher files a behavior plan with the principal. Rules for student behavior in common areas of the building have been developed jointly by the principal, teachers, and students (as appropriate) and made available to all parents and students. The principal is consistent and cooperative in implementing the school behavior plan.

5. In addition to individual classroom behavior plans and rules for student behavior in common areas of the building, a buildingwide behavior plan has been developed in which the principal assumes a joint responsibility with all staff members, students, and parents for discipline and school behavior. A climate of mutual respect exists between students, teachers, and principal based on the fair application of the plan.

Key Points in Descriptors

1. No classroom plans, no school rules, no schoolwide plan, no principal support

2. No classroom plans, no school rules, no schoolwide plan, some principal support

3. Classroom plans, school rules, no schoolwide plan, adequate principal support

4. Classroom plans, school rules developed jointly and furnished to students and parents, no schoolwide plan, excellent principal support

5. Classroom plans, school rules developed jointly and furnished to students and parents, schoolwide plan developed jointly and furnished to students and parents, excellent principal support

NOTES

1. For a more complete account of La Mesa Dale's success at raising reading achievement, see *Teach Them ALL to Read: Catching the Kids Who Fall through the Cracks* (McEwan, 2002).

2. There are a variety of books that treat the storytelling aspects of culture building in the business world. If this idea is intriguing to you, check out two of them: Neuhauser (1993) and Denning (2000).

Step Four: Communicate the Vision and Mission of Your School

The literature often uses the terms *vision* and *mission* interchangeably, but considering them as separate variables can help instructional leaders communicate both of them in more meaningful ways to staff, students, and parents.

I define *vision* as a driving force reflecting instructional leaders' image of the future, based on their values, beliefs and experiences. Descriptors such as universal, immeasurable, an object of the imagination, and unusual discernment or foresight come to mind. Vision is a personal view that provides a more global overview. *Mission*, on the other hand, is the direction that emerges from the vision and guides the day-to-day behavior of the organization. The mission, in order to be fully realized, must be developed collectively with your staff and community. Descriptors such as measurable, obtainable, purposeful, directional, ultimate goal, and commitment come to mind when reflecting on the concept of mission.

> Mission starts with determining what you really care about and want to accomplish, and committing yourself to it. You can always develop expertise. First, discover your preference.
>
> (Garfield, 1986, p. 96)

When you are hired for a principalship, whether it be your first or your fifth, you must have a clear vision for what your school (or any school) should be and can become at some time in the future. Your personal vision is based on your values, your knowledge base, and your certainty that the future state you envision will be a far better one than where the school presently is. Because you are the instructional leader, you have the responsibility for having a vision. The absence of a vision leaves you vulnerable to being what I call a chameleon leader. The chameleon leader is as adaptable as a one-size-fits-all pair of socks—no definition, no limits, and no parameters. Just tell me what you want and I'll do it.

In the beginning of any new principalship, your vision may be yours alone. You may have shared it with a committee or the superintendent during the interview process. However, all of us continually refine our vision of what schools can become, so do not make the mistake of thinking that if you did not speak up at the beginning of your principalship, you have lost the opportunity to make a difference. If not now, then when? When you are able to articulate your vision in a clear and defensible way, share key ideas and concepts with faculty members. Then encourage them to read research and think pieces that expand their horizons, send them to conferences, and bring in outside speakers. Explain the values—what you believe to be important about teaching and learning—that sustain and support your vision. As the personal visions of your faculty begin to align with your vision, you will be ready to move to the next step—writing a building mission statement.

The mission statement will not be yours alone, however; it will belong to the school community. It will incorporate the collective vision of everyone and will be a consensus statement of where you want to go together. It must be attainable in the short term and must be measurable in some way. Out of the mission statement will flow goals, objectives, and action plans that will lead to the ultimate accomplishment of the mission.

HOW CAN YOU DEVELOP COMMUNICATION CHANNELS TO SHARE THE VISION AND MISSION?

There are three audiences that need to endorse and embrace your vision if they are to commit to the task of developing a meaningful and measurable mission statement: (a) teachers, (b) parents, and (c) students. Every single member of each of these groups does not need to subscribe to the essence of your vision in order for a meaningful mission to be developed. However, key communicators and a critical mass of each group must be on board in order to achieve a mission.

Communicating Your Vision to Teachers

The work lives of teachers will change dramatically with the adoption of a new mission statement. At the outset, they may not be able to foresee the benefits that will accrue from these changes. Your job as an instructional leader is to continually explain, teach, share, demonstrate, model, facilitate, persuade, and cajole. No matter how charismatic your communication style, however, you will never convince every naysayer or change every bad attitude. Don't worry; it's not personal. These "yes-butters" never buy change. They are still using rotary dial phones and refuse to get an answering machine. Concentrate your communication efforts on the 80 percent of your staff members that respond to clear explanations, trustworthy research, definitive data, and results.

> A leader is a juggler, a person who maintains a dynamic vision of "what could be" while dealing with the everyday "what is" crises and mundane demands.
>
> (Matusak & Young, 1997, p. 51)

Open-Door Policy

Effective instructional leaders never, or rarely ever, close their doors. Even though they may be knee-deep in paperwork or problems, their body language says, "C'mon in, how can I help you?" Only salespersons need appointments with instructional leaders. All others are welcome at any time. Effective instructional leaders close their doors only when they are conferencing with students, parents, or teachers. They never close their doors to work.

Arrive First; Leave Last

Effective instructional leaders seem to live in their school buildings. They are available both early and late to share concerns, laugh over a humorous happening during the school day, or brainstorm a solution to a problem.

Dialogue, Dialogue, Dialogue

There is no substitute for good conversation, and effective instructional leaders are constantly engaged in dialogue with teachers. When teachers aren't talking, instructional leaders are out and about asking questions that will get the conversation flowing. They are talking about research, teaching, learning, and finding new ways every day to make sure that teachers share the vision and mission of the school.

> The principal is the "high priest," the one who seeks to define, strengthen, and articulate those enduring values, beliefs and cultural strands that give the school its identity.
>
> (Sergiovanni, 1984, p. 9)

The Grapevine

Every instructional leader has an informal communication network in place, an early warning system, if you will, that sends up signals about major problems looming on the horizon. Often a well-placed word or action on the part of the instructional leader can head off these major problems.

Social Events and TGIFs

All instructional leaders have their own philosophy about partying with the staff, but attending social events does offer an opportunity to get to know teachers outside the school structure. Your ability to attend these events may be a function of the size of your school. The principal of a small elementary school will have far fewer invitations than will the principal of a large high school with close to 150 staff members. I personally made an exception about attending weddings. It was well known among my staff that my husband hated weddings, and I made it a policy from the very beginning to send regrets along with a generous gift and a warm letter. The policy was accepted because I was consistent in its implementation. Of the at-least 25 or 30 weddings that took place during my principalship, I didn't attend one. Baby showers were a different matter, however. I was always there with another gift and played all the games with gusto. Crashing staff-only parties is a no-no, of course. Don't nurse hurt feelings if you're not invited. Everyone needs to let their hair down once in a while, including teachers.

Visible Presence in the Building

Research shows us that apart from anything else (e.g., what you say, what you do, or how you look), just being present in a place or at an event has an enormous impact on how teachers and students conduct themselves. Your presence notches up teaching, improves conduct, and puts everyone on their good behavior.

Daily, Weekly Faculty Bulletins

> The practice of leadership requires, perhaps first and foremost, a sense of purpose—the capacity to find the values that make risk-taking meaningful. . . . Preserving a sense of purpose helps one take setbacks and failures in stride. Leadership requires the courage to face failures daily.
>
> (Heifetz, 1994, p. 273-4)

When I was a building principal, this communication vehicle consistently got rave reviews. Each Monday morning, the faculty received a communiqué with a calendar of weekly events, summaries of any important meetings that had been held the week before, information that was needed to get through the week, accolades for staff that had made contributions in the prior week, personal thoughts on teaching and learning from the principal, and a humorous note to keep us laughing.

Occasional Lunches With Teachers

I am all in favor of putting in an occasional appearance in the teachers' lounge during lunch periods. Once a week is often enough, however. Again, as with parties, I believe staff members need 30 minutes to relax with their colleagues. The presence of the principal, albeit one with tremendous relationships with all staff members, sets a different tone for the lunch period. Tom Giles, an outstanding high school principal, disagrees with me. He believes the faculty cafeteria is "the" place to eat.

Building Leadership Teams (Curriculum Council, Management Team, Site-Based Team)

These small groups are invaluable as communication channels and decision-making vehicles for the building principal. They are usually organized in such a way that faculty feel free to bring any concerns (instructional or otherwise) to them. The teams, in turn, discuss and make recommendations to the faculty. The instructional leader who has not had the opportunity to work with a team of teachers to implement school improvement initiatives has missed one of the most energizing experiences of the principalship. Instructional leadership can be shared, and teams of teachers are perfect places to begin the sharing. Make sure that minutes of team meetings are made available to all faculty members. It's easy for the Building Team to become the haves when it comes to the inside story and the rest of the staff the have-nots.

Staff Meetings

These once-monthly (or more often) meetings are perfect vehicles for engaging in all kinds of sharing sessions and group processes. Don't let your faculty meetings become boring recitations of management items that could easily be read by everyone in the faculty bulletin. And don't let them become vehicles for complaining

> Articulating a theme, reminding people of the theme, and helping people to apply the theme to interpret their work—all are major tasks of administrators.
>
> (Weick, 1982, p. 675)

and whining. Use them to do the important work of staff development, coming to consensus on mission statements, discussing how to meet the needs of target students, ironing out conflicts, and celebrating successes.

Team, Department, or Grade-Level Meetings

Meet with these small groups on a regular basis. Take your laptop or handheld organizer along with you to take notes. You will no doubt come away with several ideas to ponder and a to-do list. Your presence will energize and refocus the group. Your reiteration of the mission and vision of the school will encourage and renew group members.

Surveys, Force Field Analyses

You should never assume that no news is good news. Effective instructional leaders are constantly "dip-sticking" the school community to make sure that everyone is focused on the goals. Simple surveys during the school year, like "What are we doing at Waterbrook School that we should keep doing?" and "What are we doing at Waterbrook School that isn't effective?" will send the message to your staff that you want to hear all the news—not just the good stuff. A helpful group process technique to use if a problem looms large on the horizon is the force field analysis. As you consider a goal or mission in the future, ask staff members to brainstorm all the positive forces that will contribute to reaching that goal. Also ask participants to list a variety of negative or restraining forces that are acting as barriers to achieving the goal. A process such as this can help identify communication or other types of barriers that are standing in your way. Many instructional leaders use a formal survey every 3 or 4 years to get a comprehensive look at how the system is functioning.

> **MUST-READ BOOKS TO ASSIST YOU IN IMPLEMENTING STEP FOUR**
>
> E. B. Goldring & S. F. Rallis. (1993). *Principals of Dynamic Schools: Taking Charge of Change.* Thousand Oaks, CA: Corwin.
>
> R. D. Ramsey. (1999). *Lead, Follow, or Get Out of the Way: How to Be a More Effective Leader in Today's Schools.* Thousand Oaks, CA: Corwin.

Communicating the Meaning and Value of Learning to Students

Do not overlook the importance of communicating the mission of the school to students. Enlist them in your cause. Give them a worthy goal, and throw in some of what Dave Burton calls the "three F's" (food, fun, and friends) to motivate their participation.

A Visible Presence

> [The principal's] belief that all students can and will learn permeates the school environment and contributes to the success of their schools.
>
> (Arthur Andersen LLP, 1997, p. 24)

Your visible presence where students are concerned is just as important as it is for teachers. Strong instructional leaders can be seen wherever students are congregated: playgrounds, athletic events, concerts and plays, bus stops, cafeterias, and hallways. Interact with individual students by name if you are able, but even if you say nothing at all and merely smile and wave, your friendly presence will communicate to students that they are important to you and that you care about their learning, their behavior, and their lives.

Opportunities at All-School Assemblies to Talk About Learning

Effective instructional leaders never miss an opportunity to share an important idea or concept with students. Whenever students are gathered together for assemblies or special events, you will hear effective instructional leaders talking about the importance of achievement, the excitement of learning, the importance of listening, or any of a dozen themes that run through principals' conversations with students.

All-School Assembly at the Beginning of the School Year

Many instructional leaders kick off every school year with an assembly that sets the tone and focus for the year. Just as the opening institute day or faculty meeting is designed to set the course for the teachers, the all-school assembly sends the message to students. It can include music, entertainment, a speech by the principal, or skits by teachers or students. Whatever the theme, it offers another opportunity to share the value and meaning of learning with students.

Be a Role Model

Effective instructional leaders model a love of learning during every school day. They can be seen reading stories aloud in classrooms and libraries, curled up on a pillow in a classroom reading their favorite novel, writing in a journal with a group of high school students, or sharing slides from their vacation trip in a history class. They can be seen using reference books and computers in the library, and talking with students about how they designed a certain lab experiment.

Small-Group Interaction

Instructional leaders take advantage of being with small groups of students to communicate ideas and goals on a more personal basis. Some schools have teacher advisory periods, and principals take their turns facilitating discussions and sharing ideas.

Written Communication

Many instructional leaders have suggestion boxes where students can leave notes, or large chart pads where students can write and principals can respond. Subjects range from the fare in the cafeteria to grades on the last social studies test.

Informal Conversation and Cafeteria Discussions

Effective instructional leaders seek out informal conversations with students whenever possible. They are good communicators with students—in tune with the music, the books, the clothes, and the interests of their particular age group.

Academic Communication

Commending students for outstanding achievement, listening to students read books aloud or share their writing, and sending personal notes to students who appear in newspaper articles are just some of the ways principals reinforce and commend learning.

Instructional leaders have a clear vision of what the school is trying to accomplish. . . . Out of this sense of mission evolves a sense of purpose shared by the staff, students, and community.

(Hallinger & Murphy, 1987, p. 57)

Hot Off the Press

Effective instructional leaders never miss an opportunity to let the rest of the community know what is happening in their schools. They publish honor rolls, submit articles about special achievements, and feature students of the week and month in a special column.

Student Council

Just as instructional leaders use building-leadership teams to establish solid, two-way communication channels between faculty and principal, they use student council as a way to build communication with students. Student councils are marvelous vehicles for enlisting student support for projects like building cleanup, recycling, or fundraising for new library books or athletic equipment.

School Newspaper or Magazine

A student-run newspaper or magazine is another important vehicle for finding out what is important to students. Editorials and news articles should be carefully read and problems responded to with care and diplomacy.

Television

Many schools use the resources of in-house television to create their own in-school news broadcast each day. Instructional leaders frequently broadcast messages to students. Use these opportunities to appear on TV to reiterate the vision and mission of your school. Find new ways to communicate the mission—through object lessons, humorous stories, or visuals.

Community Resources

If students have an opportunity to hear from graduates about the importance of learning, the impact can be powerful. We invited community members to our school to read aloud during a special week each year. But we also asked them to specifically talk about the importance of reading in their career. The fire chief brought in his manuals and policies. The electrician brought in his diagrams and schematics. The school superintendent even brought in his board policies and professional journals. It was just another way of communicating the importance of learning to students.

Getting Parents On Board

Invite parents to join your learning community. You will find them eager participants and supportive with both their time and money, if you only give them a chance. Make them feel welcome. Invite them to share their problems and concerns with you. Don't run the other way when you see a parent coming. Use the opportunity to build support for your school mission.

Classroom Letters to Parents

Encourage classroom teachers to write weekly or monthly letters to parents. This is a powerful way to communicate to them what is happening at school. These letters might give ideas about activities for parents and students to do together or, in the case of high school students, provide tips about college scholarships or applications.

Weekly (Monthly) Parent Letter

Many instructional leaders write a weekly or monthly parent letter. It may or may not be part of a newsletter. It usually focuses on some aspect of learning and encourages parents to follow practices at home that support what the school is doing.

> The community may provide a frame of reference for defining a school's mission, but it is the leaders' visions that guide the day-to-day functioning of schools.
>
> (Weber, 1987, p. 13)

Informal Cottage Coffees

Small groups of parents who gather in one individual's home for a morning or evening coffee can be a good communication channel. Teachers, and perhaps the principal, mingle informally with parents or, possibly, make a brief presentation. These informal gatherings allow for different kinds of conversational exchanges than might occur in the more formal school setting. Some schools plan early breakfasts for moms and dads who work outside the home.

Parent Involvement and Advisory Organizations

Every school needs a formal parent organization that allows all parents the opportunity to be involved in some way at school. Instructional leaders are skilled at working with these groups to achieve school goals and recognize the power that exists in an organized parent group. They meet with them informally to plan agendas and set goals, and they attend all the business meetings. Wise instructional leaders use the parent organization for more than just fundraising. They tap the collective wisdom of the group for accomplishing the school mission.

Homework Hotlines

Many instructional leaders have found ways to use technology to communicate with parents. One of the most popular ways is a homework hotline. Parents can keep in touch with teachers and monitor their students' progress with only the press of a button. This program is very popular with parents.

Web Sites

Many schools have comprehensive Web sites, and I can attest to their helpfulness when looking for a phone number, the name of an administrator, a map, or a date for some upcoming function. Use Web sites to publish school improvement news and test data.

Newspaper Column

Writing a weekly newspaper column is another way that some instructional leaders communicate with parents. The column can feature school events, accomplishments of individual students, book reviews of outstanding reading for children, answers to questions that parents often ask, or advice about parenting issues. While the deadline of a weekly column is often a pressure for the busy instructional leader, the payback in terms of public relations and communication is incredible.

Family Learning Events

Invite parents to school to share learning experiences with children. Engage in hands-on science or math activities; dance the Virginia reel in gym class; or do an art project together. These activities do more than just showcase your school; they model for parents how to learn with their children.

Back-to-School Nights

These traditional open houses permit parents to walk through their child's school day. They give parents a feel for the teachers, the classrooms, and the expectations for their child. They are important vehicles for communicating the mission of the school to parents. Gathering all the parents together in one location prior to moving from classroom to classroom is a technique that many instructional leaders use. It is yet another opportunity to articulate for parents what our school is all about.

School Newspaper

Student-produced newspapers are common at the high school level, but they can also serve as important channels of communication at the junior high and elementary levels. The school newspaper contains material written by and for students but is sent to parents and shows parents the quality of work that students are producing in the school.

School Newsletter

This is an important communication vehicle at any grade level, but it is especially important at the junior high and high school levels when parent involvement, and frequently even interest, may fall off sharply. The newsletter can contain schedules of special events, news of students' achievements, articles about new curricular offerings, and a special column or letter of greeting from the principal.

Parent-Teacher Conferences

These yearly, or sometimes twice-yearly, events are one of the most important communication events between parent and school. The focus is on the individual children, their needs, their strengths, and their academic progress. Instructional leaders spend time in helping all teachers structure effective conferences but particularly focus on new staff members.

Informal Visits to Homes

While home visits are time-consuming, they can be extraordinarily beneficial for building rapport and strong relationships between the home and school. While many districts use parent facilitators in preschool programs, home visits in upper grades are not as common as they used to be. Instructional leaders who are able to include them in their repertoire of communication channels are enthusiastic about the benefits.

HOW CAN YOU USE THE INSTRUCTIONAL LEADERSHIP CHECKLIST TO ASSESS STEP FOUR?

Step Four: Communicate the Vision and Mission of Your School

There are three indicators that describe this step in more detail. Each indicator is followed by three sections: (a) a *comment* that defines the specific focus of the indicator; (b) a *scale of descriptors* that gives a continuum of behaviors (1 to 5) from least effective to most effective; and (c) *key points in the descriptors* that give succinct explanations of each of the five items in the scale. For each indicator, select the number from 1 to 5 that most accurately describes your own behavior on a day-to-day basis.

Indicator 4.1

Provides for systematic two-way communication with staff regarding the achievement standards and the improvement goals of the school.

Comment

The main focus of Indicator 4.1 is the provision of two-way communication channels to ensure an ongoing discussion of the mission of the school.

Scale of Descriptors

1. There is no communication between principal and staff regarding the mission of the school.

2. Communication between principal and staff is largely one way and limited to administrative directives regarding principal expectations.

3. Although principal and staff communicate informally regarding the mission of the school, there are no regular two-way communication channels.

4. Two-way communication channels between principal and staff have been established in the form of faculty meetings; grade-level, departmental, and team meetings; and teacher and principal conferences; but these channels are frequently used for administrative or social purposes and are not regularly devoted to a discussion of instructional goals and priorities.

5. Established two-way communication channels are regularly used by the principal as a means of addressing the standards and improvement goals of the school with the staff.

Key Points in Descriptors

1. No communication

2. One-way communication, no established channels

3. Informal two-way communication, no established channels

4. Established channels, no regular use of these channels

5. Regular use of established channels for two-way communication regarding school mission

Indicator 4.2

Establishes, supports, and implements activities that communicate the value and meaning of learning to students.

Comment

The main focus of Indicator 4.2 is the existence of activities that communicate the value of learning to students. Examples of such activities might be awards or honors assemblies, learning-incentive programs, career awareness programs, honor societies, work-study programs, academic clubs, and mentoring or shadowing programs. This list is meant to be suggestive but certainly not inclusive.

Scale of Descriptors

1. No activities exist that communicate the value and meaning of learning to students.

2. At least one activity exists that communicates the value and meaning of learning to students.

3. More than three activities exist that communicate the value and meaning of learning to students.

4. More than six activities exist that communicate the value and meaning of learning to students.

5. More than 10 activities exist that communicate the value and meaning of learning to students.

Key Points in Descriptors

1. No activities

2. One activity

3. More than three activities

4. More than six activities

5. More than 10 activities

Indicator 4.3

Develops and uses communication channels with parents to set forth school objectives.

Comment

The main focus of Indicator 4.3 is the existence of communication channels that are specifically devoted to setting forth standards and school improvement goals to parents. Examples of communication channels might include, but not necessarily be limited to, grade-level curriculum nights; newsletter column devoted specifically to school objectives; parent conferences; written statement of school mission; written statement of standards for each grade level, particularly in the core curricular areas of reading and mathematics; school activities devoted to skill mastery that require parent participation (e.g., contract for parents reading with or aloud to students); and homework policy.

Scale of Descriptors

1. No communication channels to setting forth school objectives exist.

2. At least three communication channels exist to setting forth school objectives.

3. At least six communication channels exist to setting forth school objectives.

4. At least 10 communication channels exist to setting forth school objectives.

5. In addition to the 10 communication channels that exist to setting forth school objectives, the principal and faculty are evaluating, refining, and developing additional means of communicating with parents regarding school objectives.

Key Points in Descriptors

1. No channels

2. At least three channels

3. At least six channels

4. At least 10 channels

5. At least 10 channels and an evaluation, refining, and development process

Step Five: Set High Expectations for Your Staff and Yourself

Step five is about notching up the instructional performance of your teachers while at the same time fine-tuning your personal instructional leadership capabilities. This aspect of instructional leadership is the most time-consuming and emotionally demanding of any of the seven steps. It is, however, critical to the creation of a true learning community. Heifetz (1994) summarized the challenge when he said, "Leadership . . . requires a learning strategy. A leader has to engage people in facing the challenge, adjusting their values, changing perspectives, and developing new habits of behavior" (p. 276). Strong instructional leaders don't just tell—they model, demonstrate, and show the way.

HOW CAN YOU SET HIGH EXPECTATIONS FOR TEACHERS?

Setting high expectations for teachers means "knowing what a good one looks like." Teaching is an enormously complex behavior, and setting high expectations is not a task for the faint of

> A good principal does not tolerate bad teachers.
>
> (Keller, 1998, p. 26)

heart. Instructional leaders must establish a standard of excellence in teaching, define benchmarks of instructional effectiveness, and then do everything imaginable to help teachers meet that standard and reach those benchmarks. The same tensions that exist in setting high expectations for students can plague instructional leaders as they work with teachers. How can you provide outstanding clinical supervision and coaching in an environment that calls for strict evaluation and assessment? How can you work collegially with teachers within the context of a negotiated contract? Somehow, effective instructional leaders are able to manage this high-wire act. They have learned to move artlessly between supervision and evaluation, letting teachers know they believe in them and will help them reach their personal and professional goals.

HOW CAN YOU ASSIST TEACHERS IN SETTING GOALS?

Assisting teachers in setting personal and professional goals is about making everything we know about effective instruction part of our school culture and climate. Helping teachers set personal and professional goals is a tricky task for instructional leaders, however. A staff of 30 may have beginners and veterans, subject matter specialists and generalists, as well as right-brained and left-brained learners. Instructional leaders must be flexible enough to match the personal and professional goals to the individual teacher, skillful enough to bring the best out in everyone. Chris Gaylord is particularly effective in this area. She helps all the teachers to set individual goals based on talent, commitment, and the reality of their particular life situation.

Sister Catherine Wingert helps her teachers tie their personal goals to the building goals, thus avoiding fragmentation and lack of focus. Paul Zaander asks his staff to develop goals that relate to instructional improvement in both their classrooms and the school community. Effective instructional leaders model goal setting by publicly sharing their personal goals with the staff. This public baring of the soul serves two purposes: (a) it holds the administrators accountable before their staff for accomplishment of the goal; and (b) it offers a positive role model for risk taking and self-improvement.

Stella Loeb-Munson encourages her teachers to set professional goals that reach beyond the classroom. She focuses on presentation skills and showcasing their expertise in contests and award competitions, while Linda Hanson encourages teachers to write books and do original research. If a goal is to have meaning and worth, accountability with regard to its completion is essential. Strong instructional leaders meet once or twice per year with each teacher to receive an update on goal progress. As the year draws to a close, progress is summarized, and goals for the following year are discussed.

Critical to any self-improvement effort that you ask teachers to undertake, however, is their inner willingness to change. Change imposed from the outside is seldom meaningful.

You can gain leverage in motivating teachers to change if they are able to observe you setting goals and changing your behaviors (e.g., setting a goal to be a more visible presence in the building and doing it, or setting a goal to increase the number of classrooms visited each day and achieving it); the goal-setting process will have more meaning and relevance to them. Actions always are more impressive and long lasting than verbiage.

Community High School
(continued)

history, we want to see a solid core of upper-level courses in that department.

There is one question that Alan never fails to explore in the interview process: Do the candidates have a deep understanding of their subject? He explains:

One question that we often use in interviews comes out of the recent national discussions about U.S. math curriculum— "a mile wide and an inch deep." We'll ask, for example, "If you [the candidate] had to get rid of three topics from the curriculum in your discipline (e.g., algebra, biology, American history), what would they be?" Another, related question we might ask is, "Name one topic in your discipline that you would die for." The basic question I am exploring is, "What knowledge is of most worth to you?"

Alan expects the teachers he hires to have the answers to the National Research Council questions (cited in Chapter 1) on the tips of their tongues. As Alan concludes, "If prospective American history teachers can't tell me what's essential in the study of American history, how can they be effective American history teachers?" At other high schools in the area, most of them with more privileged students, whether teacher candidates can coach baseball or women's basketball along with teaching history or math may be the reason they get hired, but in Alan's mind, coaching and content don't mix.

WHERE CAN YOU FIND THE TIME?

The question of how principals spend their time is a function not only of what they are expected to do but also of the tasks and responsibilities they value most. Krajewski (1978) found that secondary school principals placed the highest value on instructional leadership activities and the lowest value on tasks in the management area. However, when their values were compared to the way they actually spent their time, there was a large discrepancy. Later research by Smith and Andrews (1989) compared the way average instructional leaders (as perceived by their teaching staff) spent their time versus strong instructional leaders (as perceived by their teaching staff). Strong instructional leaders spent their time quite differently from average principals. Average principals believed they *should* allocate the greatest percentage of the time to educational program improvement, but in reality, they spent far more time on management and student services. Excellent instructional leaders, however, accomplished the management tasks in a similar time frame as the average instructional leader but spent far less time on student-related activities. Strong instructional leaders value educational improvement activities, manage their time wisely to accomplish these tasks, and still find time to get everything else done.

How do they do it? "I don't find the time—I make time! Each month on my desk calendar, I pencil in teachers and classes to observe, usually two per day." Effective instructional leaders make classroom visits and observations an absolute priority. "I do not schedule anything during the school day that can be held before or after school, in order to make classroom visits my priority." They are adamant about the need to allocate time. "You must place your observations on your calendar and treat them the same way you'd treat an appointment with your superintendent." Another instructional leader put it this way: "I schedule the observations and ask

---

Before principals envision or mandate changes for others, they benefit from looking at and understanding how their own expectations of themselves as leaders may help or hinder their leadership in action.

(Ackerman, Donaldson, & van der Bogert, 1996, p. 101)

GOAL SETTING EVERY 30 DAYS: KATHIE DOBBERTEEN, PRINCIPAL

La Mesa Dale Elementary School, La Mesa, California

The typical goal-setting cycle in the average school is yearly. Kathie Dobberteen and her staff have tightened up that cycle and work from month to month. This 30-day cycle has several advantages: (a) Focus and motivation are maintained; (b) accountability is never lost; (c) teachers, students, and parents can see short-term results; and (d) goals are always meaningful and measurable. Schmoker (1999) shared the basic concepts of *rapid results* and *30-minute meetings* as tools for increasing achievement in La Mesa-Spring Valley School District. Christopher Quinn, a former principal in the

(continued)

my secretary not to interrupt for anything short of someone dying." They use a variety of techniques to keep organized. Some keep clipboards or journals. Some put their observations on the calendar during the month of August and work everything else around them, rather than making the observations fit in the schedule. They communicate to everyone—secretaries, teachers, parents, and even the superintendent—that classroom observations, are a priority and they will not be interrupted.

HOW CAN OBSERVATION AND FEEDBACK BE USED?

The types of observation and data-collecting procedures principals use are often mandated by the settings in which they work. The instruments, the methodologies, the length of observations, and the frequency of pre- and post-conferences are often dictated by the negotiated contract or district policies. Regardless of the methodologies they use, however, effective instructional

> **La Mesa Dale Elementary School** (continued)
>
> district, then designed and fine-tuned a rapid-results, 30-minute, 30-day, goal-setting process (McEwan, 2002). Under Kathie's strong instructional leadership, this process has provided the power to fuel skyrocketing achievement. Here's how it works. For example, the second-grade team might meet to examine the results of a recent fluency test given to their students. They would then decide on a 30-day goal to increase the fluency rates of every student regardless of reading level. Before they leave the 30-minute meeting, they have put together an action plan to accomplish the goal, assumed responsibilities for various tasks, and agreed on a date for a meeting in 30 days. The teachers know that both their plan *and* the 30-day results will be shared with Kathie, and they are committed to working together to achieve their collaborative goal.

leaders are in almost universal agreement that observation and feedback are near the top of the list when it comes to ways for improving instruction (Guzzetti & Martin, 1984). Unfortunately, that's not how many principals spend their time (Morris, Crowson, Hurwitz, & Porter-Gehrie, 1982). If principals believe that observation and feedback are critical, why don't they do it more regularly?

- Quality teacher observations are time-consuming.
- Quality teacher observations require confidence in one's own teaching knowledge and skills.
- Providing quality feedback, especially in the context of teacher evaluation, is difficult and stressful—for both the teacher and the principal.

Conducting high-level observations and structuring meaningful feedback sessions are comparable to the activities of working out and eating healthily. We all know how good the latter are for us, but they

MUST-READ BOOKS TO ASSIST YOU IN IMPLEMENTING STEP FIVE

S. C. Carter. (1999). *No Excuses: Seven Principals of Low-Income Schools Who Set the Standard for High Achievement.* Washington, DC: The Heritage Foundation.

T. R. Guskey. (2000). *Evaluating Professional Development.* Thousand Oaks, CA: Corwin.

B. Joyce & B. Showers. (1995). *Student Achievement Through Staff Development.* New York: Longman.

E. K. McEwan. (2001). *Ten Traits of Highly Effective Teachers: How to Hire, Mentor and Coach Successful Teachers.* Thousand Oaks, CA: Corwin.

J. Saphier & R. Gower. (1997). *The Skillful Teacher: Building Your Teaching Skills.* Acton, MA: Research for Better Teaching.

require discipline, structure, organization, commitment, skill, and some sacrifice. Concomitantly, we all know how beneficial observation and feedback are to the improvement of instruction, but they also require discipline, structure, organization, commitment, skill, and some sacrifice.

In order to provide feedback that has any likelihood of improving teachers' effectiveness, instructional leaders must first have a solid knowledge base regarding instructional strategies and models. Second, they must be able to use and explain to teachers a variety of data collection processes, for example, time-on-task or the ratio of praise to criticism. During the observation process, intense concentration, penetrating analytical skills, and the ability to capture both minute detail and the big picture in a written form are some of the requirements for super-principal. Once data has been observed, collected, and analyzed, the task has only just begun. The most crucial aspect of teacher observation and evaluation is the sharing of feedback in a collegial manner that facilitates open discussion and leads the teachers to reflect on their teaching. Bird and Little (1985) call this "reciprocity" and suggest a five-point standard for principal and teachers to follow to ensure that observations result in the improvement of instruction and hence increased learning by students:

1. The principal must promise to bring knowledge and skill to the observation in order to help the teacher.

2. The teachers must acknowledge that they have something to learn from hearing the principals discuss their teaching.

3. The principals must demonstrate a certain level of skill and knowledge so as to give credibility to their statements about the teacher's performance.

4. The principal must be able to provide the teacher with one or more of the following: some type of detailed recording of the observation (coded chart, script-tape, etc.); an idea or suggestion of some alternative practice that would be more effective than what the teacher was doing; a

detailed description about what was outstanding in the lesson; and, in some cases, a personally taught lesson so the observer could watch the principal.

5. The teachers must try to change their teaching practices in response to the observation and evaluation.

Principals have an obligation to improve their observation and conferencing skills at the same time that they are expecting their teachers to improve instruction. Perhaps a concrete example will more clearly illuminate the meaning of reciprocity. As a beginning principal, I was eager to acquire skills in observing and conferencing. I went to workshops, enrolled in administrators' academies, and practiced. The district in which I worked hired a consultant to provide assistance in clinical supervision for anyone who was interested, and I eagerly volunteered. The consultant and I observed a lesson together. The consultant then observed me conferencing with that teacher. We worked from a shared knowledge base about what had happened during the lesson. The consultant then conferred with me regarding my conference with the teacher. This was such a successful experience, I invited several brave teachers to try other variations with me. I taught a lesson and one of my teachers observed and conferred with me. One of my teachers and I observed a lesson together and she observed me conferring with the teacher and gave me feedback. Then, in a moment of insane risk taking, I volunteered myself and a staff member for the ultimate in a public display of teaching and conferencing. We bused an entire class of sixth graders and their teacher to a local university where over 100 principals observed her teaching a math lesson. The principals recorded their data and personally evaluated her lesson. I then participated in a panel with several other principals to talk about how we would have conferred with the teacher. Reciprocity simply means remaining vulnerable and open to taking risks as an individual; it means that you, the principal, will never forget how personal the act of teaching often is, and that you will continually grow and change yourself as a professional.

WHAT ARE THE BEST CONFERENCING TECHNIQUES?

Effective instructional leaders spend a great deal of time and energy on observations and conferences. Merry Gayle Wade describes the process she uses:

> I have an observational conference after each of my classroom visits. Before I go into the classroom, I decide what the focus of the

visit will be. I take careful notes and write only what I saw, not what I think should have happened. After returning from the observations, I take a little time to review my notes and decide what I can share with teachers to help them become more effective. I begin each conference by letting the teachers know I always enjoy visiting their class and ask how they felt about the lesson. This usually gets me in the improvement mode. When the teacher leaves my office, I hope I have given them at least one idea they can use to improve their instruction. I believe teachers really want their administrators to know what they're doing. They want to be recognized for the difficult job they do. I see myself as a coach trying to lead the team into a winning year.

Stella Loeb-Munson focuses every conference on the instructional process with one goal in mind—improvement of instruction. She asks these questions in every conference, and although they remain the same, the discussions and shared knowledge are different every time:

- Were the best of all possible choices for instruction in evidence?
- Were learning principles addressed and served to the benefit of every student?
- Did all students become involved and enthusiastic about their own learning?
- Did the goals set for the lesson happen? Why? Why not?
- How can we make this better?
- What do we add, take out, modify?
- What did you like best?
- What would you change? Why?

WHAT IS THE IMPORTANCE OF DIRECT TEACHING?

Effective instructional leaders recognize the value, both practical and symbolic, of engaging in direct teaching themselves. They feel that teaching in the classroom gives them an opportunity to show staff and students that they are first a teacher and second a principal. "I love the excitement generated by human beings learning and enjoying the process while they're doing it." Another shared, "It gives principals an opportunity to model what they preach. It shows teachers that you are still a teacher, and it shows the students that you can still do it." Gary Catalani uses his teaching as a reward in a monthly drawing he holds with teachers. Two teachers receive a half-day release time. Gary teaches these classes while the teachers engage in other professional activities.

HOW CAN YOU SET HIGH EXPECTATIONS FOR YOURSELF?

Setting high expectations for teachers while failing to do the same for oneself is an exercise in hypocrisy. How can any instructional leader reasonably expect teachers to set goals, be evaluated regularly, accept feedback on their performance, and continually grow as a professional if the principal is not willing to do the same? Strong instructional leaders regularly solicit performance feedback from their staff members, use that feedback to set goals, and share those goals with staff members in anticipation of a new cycle of performance, evaluation, and feedback.

In the spring of each year, I asked my staff members to complete a short, three-question evaluation related to my job performance that school year:

> The individual has within himself vast resources for self-understanding, for altering his self-concept, his attitudes, and his self-directed behavior. . . . These resources can be tapped only [if] a definable climate of facilitative psychological attitudes can be provided.
>
> (Rogers, 1974, p. 115)

1. What am I doing as an instructional leader that is contributing to the mission of our school and to your effectiveness as a teacher (office personnel, instructional aide, lunchroom or playground supervisor, etc.)?

2. What am I doing that is standing in the way of your effectiveness in your job role?

3. What would you like me to start doing that I am not currently doing that would enable you to be a more effective teacher (aide, secretary, health worker, etc.)?

I asked the building leadership team to collate the responses and then select a representative from the group who would be comfortable sharing the results (both the good news and the bad) with me. I used this feedback to evaluate my own performance and to set goals for the coming year. On one occasion, I used an instrument developed by Andrews and Soder for their study of strong and weak instructional leaders in Seattle, Washington (Andrews, 1989; Andrews & Soder, 1987). Each staff member completed a questionnaire that was collected and mailed to Andrews, who had been hired by the Illinois Principals Association to work with our membership on instructional leadership issues. I was then privileged to meet with Andrews to discuss the results of my evaluation. This process illuminated for me how often we principals convince ourselves that we are doing things that we really aren't. Or at least our teachers perceive that we are not doing them. And teachers' perceptions of how effective we are as instructional leaders are, for them, reality.

Since the publication of the first edition of *Seven Steps to Effective Instructional Leadership*, many administrators have used all or parts of the Instructional Leadership Checklist as part of their personal evaluation process. Some have asked teachers to complete the survey; others have done a self-study. ElizaBeth McCay, an educational administration faculty member at Virginia Commonwealth University, uses the Instructional Leadership Checklist as the first assignment in her course on the principalship. Students are asked to assess and then develop a plan of improvement for one of the seven steps (or one of the indicators of one of the seven steps) in their school setting. Dr. McCay admits that this is a grueling assignment for students but that they grow tremendously from the experience. "We build in class time to share ideas for improvement so their ideas for implementation expand exponentially. Some students are already in leadership positions, so they conduct a self-assessment, with rich results. Some of the practicing administrators also survey their faculties using the instrument as well." Resource B contains Dr. McCay's assignment, a suggested format to follow, and a scoring rubric.

HOW CAN YOU USE THE INSTRUCTIONAL LEADERSHIP CHECKLIST TO ASSESS STEP FIVE?

Step Five: Set High Expectations for Your Staff and Yourself

There are seven indicators that describe this step in more detail. Each indicator is followed by three sections: (a) a *comment* that defines the specific focus of the indicator; (b) a *scale of descriptors* that gives a continuum of behaviors (1 to 5) from least effective to most effective; and (c) *key points in the descriptors* that give succinct explanations of each of the five items in the scale. For each indicator, select the number from 1 to 5 that most accurately describes your own behavior on a day-to-day basis. (District requirements for frequency and procedures with regard to teacher evaluation may vary and substantially impact the interpretation of step five. In large schools, several administrators may share supervision and evaluation responsibilities. The indicators and their scales of descriptors describes a best-case scenario.)

Indicator 5.1

Assists teachers yearly in setting and reaching personal and professional goals related to the improvement of instruction, student achievement, and professional development.

Comment

The main focus of Indicator 5.1 is the active participation of the principal with teachers in goal-setting and goal-achieving processes. The principal provides assistance to the teachers in reaching stated goals, and the information obtained in the goal-setting process is used in teacher evaluation.

Scale of Descriptors

1. Principal does not require that teachers set personal and professional goals.

2. Principal requires that all teachers develop, in cooperation with the principal, personal and professional goals but is not involved in the goal-setting process and does not require that goals be related to the improvement of instruction and overall school improvement goals.

3. Principal requires that teachers set personal and professional goals and that these goals be related to the improvement of instruction and overall school improvement goals but does not assist in the attainment of goals or monitor completion.

4. Principal requires that all teachers develop, in cooperation with the principal, personal and professional goals, and that these goals be related to the improvement of instruction and overall school improvement goals; provides assistance in the attainment of these goals.

5. Principal requires that all teachers develop, in cooperation with the principal, personal and professional goals related to the improvement of instruction and overall school improvement goals. Principal provides assistance to the teachers in the attainment of goals, monitors the completion of the goals, and uses the information in the evaluation process.

Key Points in Descriptors

1. No goal setting by teachers.

2. Goal setting not necessarily related to the improvement of instruction. No principal input, assistance, monitoring, or evaluation.

3. Goal setting related to improvement of instruction. Principal input. No principal assistance, monitoring, or evaluation.

4. Goal setting related to improvement of instruction. Principal input and assistance. No principal monitoring or evaluation.

5. Goal setting related to improvement of instruction. Principal input, assistance, monitoring, and evaluation.

Indicator 5.2

Makes regular classroom observations in all classrooms, both informal (drop-in visits of varying length with no written or verbal feedback to teacher) and formal (visits where observation data are recorded and communicated to teacher).

Comment

The main focus of Indicator 5.2 is on the quantity of classroom observations (both formal and informal).

Scale of Descriptors

1. Principal makes formal classroom observations once every 3 years or less and never visits the classroom informally.

2. Principal makes at least one formal classroom observation per year and occasionally drops in informally.

3. Principal makes two formal classroom observations per year and at least two monthly informal observations.

4. Principal makes three formal classroom observations per year and at least two monthly informal observations.

5. Principal makes four or more classroom observations per year and visits the classroom informally at least once each week.

Key Points in Descriptors

1. Minimal formal observations and no informal observations

2. One yearly formal observation and minimal informal observations

3. Two yearly formal observations and two monthly informal observations

4. Three yearly formal observations and two monthly informal observations

5. Four yearly formal observations and weekly informal observations

Indicator 5.3

Engages in planning of classroom observations.

Comment

The main focus of Indicator 5.3 is the quality of pre-observation planning for a formal classroom observation where information is collected relative to improvement of instruction.

Scale of Descriptors

1. There is no typical pattern. Teachers are not usually aware that the principal will visit.

2. The principal generally informs teachers before an observation. A lesson may be observed, but there is no specific request for such on the part of the principal.

3. The principal and teacher arrange together for a specific observation time. A complete lesson is usually observed.

4. The principal and teacher arrange together for a specific observation time. A discussion is held regarding the lesson plan for the observation, but no attempts are ever made by the principal to focus on specific curricular areas or instructional strategies (e.g., cooperative grouping in a reading lesson, questioning techniques used on target students). A complete lesson is always observed.

5. The principal and teacher plan the focus of each observation at a conference. Principal frequently takes the initiative regarding the focus of the observation and relates it to building goals and objectives. A specific observation time is scheduled. A complete lesson is always observed.

Key Points in Descriptors

1. No teacher awareness of observation. No pre-observation planning. Random observation of incomplete lessons.

2. Teacher awareness of observation. No pre-observation planning. Observation includes both complete and incomplete lessons.

3. Teacher awareness of observation. No pre-observation planning. Observation always includes complete lesson.

4. Teacher awareness of observation. Pre-observation planning without specific focus by principal. Complete lesson always observed.

5. Teacher awareness of observation. Pre-observation planning with frequent principal initiative regarding subject of observation. Complete lesson always observed.

Indicator 5.4

Engages in postobservation conferences that focus on the improvement of instruction. (District requirements for frequency and procedures with regard to teacher evaluation may vary and substantially impact the interpretation of this indicator. The scale of descriptors describes a best-case scenario.)

Comment

The main focus of Indicator 5.4 is the quantity and quality of postobservation conferences that focus on the improvement of instruction.

Scale of Descriptors

1. The principal engages in a postobservation conference once every 2 years or less with each teacher, with little to no focus on the improvement of instruction.

2. The principal engages in one postobservation conference with each teacher every year but rarely focuses on the improvement of instruction.

3. The principal engages in two postobservation conferences with each teacher every year and provides one-way information about the improvement of instruction.

4. The principal engages in three postobservation conferences with each teacher every year, engaging in both one-way and two-way communication about the improvement of instruction.

5. The principal engages in four postobservation conferences with each teacher every year, engaging in both one-way and two-way communication about the improvement of instruction. Joint plans for follow-up in the classroom are developed with principal providing instructional resources and assistance.

Key Points in Descriptors

1. One conference every 2 years with little to no focus on improvement of instruction

2. One conference every year with rare focus on improvement of instruction

3. Two conferences every year with one-way communication about improvement of instruction

4. Three conferences every year with both one-way and two-way communication about the improvement of instruction

5. Four conferences every year with both one-way and two-way communication about the improvement of instruction, and joint plans for follow-up with instructional resources and assistance provided

Indicator 5.5

Provides thorough, defensible, and insightful evaluations, making recommendations for personal- and professional-growth goals according to individual needs.

Comment

The main focus of Indicator 5.5 is the quality of the evaluation provided by the principal.

Scale of Descriptors

1. All teachers receive nearly identical written evaluation ratings from the principal. There is no indication that the evaluation is based on direct observation or supporting evidence, and no suggestions for improvement or growth are made.

2. Most teachers receive nearly identical written evaluation ratings from the principal. There is little indication that evaluation is based on direct observation or supporting evidence, and no suggestions for improvement or growth are made.

3. Although gradations of written evaluation ratings exist, these gradations appear to have no relationship to teacher performance or supporting evidence. No suggestions for improvement or growth are made.

4. Most teachers receive thorough written evaluations based on direct observation and supporting evidence. Principal makes few suggestions for improvement and growth.

5. Each teacher receives a thoughtful written evaluation based on direct observation and supporting evidence. Principal includes suggestions for improvement and growth tailored to individual needs.

Key Points in Descriptors

1. Identical evaluations for all teachers. No supporting evidence. No suggestions for growth.

2. Nearly identical evaluations for all teachers. No supporting evidence. No suggestions for growth.

3. Gradation of evaluation ratings. No supporting evidence. No suggestions for growth.

4. Thorough evaluations for all teachers. Supporting evidence. Few suggestions for growth.

5. Thorough evaluations for all teachers. Supporting evidence. Suggestions for growth.

Indicator 5.6

Engages in direct teaching in the classrooms.

Comment

The main focus of Indicator 5.6 is the number of times the principal teaches a lesson observed by a classroom teacher. This indicator does not include reading stories aloud or assisting teachers. It focuses on lesson preparation and the opportunity for the classroom teacher to engage in an observation of the principal teaching this lesson.

Scale of Descriptors

1. Principal engages in no direct teaching in the classroom.

2. Principal engages in direct teaching in any classroom at least once per year.

3. Principal engages in direct teaching in any classroom at least two to four times per year.

4. Principal engages in direct teaching in any classroom at least five to ten times per year.

5. Principal engages in direct teaching in the classroom more than 10 times per year.

Key Points in Descriptors

1. No direct teaching

2. One episode of direct teaching

3. Two to four episodes of direct teaching

4. Five to ten episodes of direct teaching

5. More than 10 episodes of direct teaching

Indicator 5.7

Principal holds high expectations for personal instructional leadership behavior, regularly solicits feedback (both formal and informal) from staff members regarding instructional leadership abilities, and uses such feedback to set yearly performance goals.

Comment

The main focus of Indicator 5.7 is the regularity with which principals solicit input from staff members regarding their own performance and the attention paid to this input with regard to goal setting and genuine attempts to change unproductive behaviors.

Scale of Descriptors

1. Principal does not consider instructional leadership a reliable construct on which to be evaluated by staff members and solicits no input from them relative to own performance.

2. Principal considers instructional leadership to be a reliable evaluative construct and occasionally solicits feedback from staff members relative to own performance but does not use this feedback to set goals.

3. Principal considers instructional leadership to be a reliable evaluative construct, solicits feedback (both formal and informal) from staff members relative to own performance, and makes sporadic attempts to use this information to set goals to change own leadership behavior.

4. Principal considers instructional leadership to be a reliable evaluative construct, solicits feedback (both formal and informal) from staff members relative to own performance, sets yearly performance goals, and can be observed by faculty regularly adding productive leadership behaviors, but is resistant to changing unproductive behaviors.

5. Principal considers instructional leadership to be a reliable evaluative construct, solicits feedback (both formal and informal) from staff members relative to own performance, sets yearly performance goals, can be observed by faculty regularly adding productive leadership behaviors and eliminating unproductive behaviors.

Key Points

1. No feedback solicited from staff members.
2. Some feedback solicited from staff members. No goal setting.
3. Feedback regularly solicited from staff members. Inconsistent use of feedback data to set goals.

4. Regular feedback. Regular goal setting. Addition of productive leadership behaviors. Resistance to elimination of unproductive behaviors.

5. Regular feedback. Regular goal setting. Addition of productive leadership behaviors. Elimination of unproductive behaviors.

Step Six: Develop Teacher Leaders

The teaching profession, by its very nature, works against the concept of teacher leaders. Lieberman (1988) calls it an "egalitarian ethic" and suggests that it almost mandates teachers to think of everyone as the same, no matter how experienced, how effective, or how knowledgeable individual teachers may be. Yet the sense of mission and passion for making a difference that drives highly effective teachers will not find its full expression until they are able to step forward and assume leadership roles.

Some teachers, however, have a difficult time seeing themselves as leaders. The hierarchical nature of the public schools is based on the 19th-century industrial model that places teachers and principals in an adversarial relationship, one that is often exacerbated at the bargaining table (Troen & Boles, 1994). Some teachers feel that the principal is in charge, and teachers should merely follow orders. They feel uncomfortable with sharing decision making and accountability, believing that those are administrative prerogatives. However, the individual who sees teaching as anything other than an opportunity to lead misses the mark completely (McEwan, 2001). The effective instructional leader cannot afford to overlook or discount the importance of mentoring teacher leaders—the mission is much too large to go it alone.

WHAT IS A TEACHER LEADER?

My own personal definition of a teacher leader is an individual who exhibits leadership skills in one or more of the following areas: (a) mentoring and coaching new teachers; (b) collaborating with all staff members (regardless of personal affiliation or preference); (c) learning and growing with a view to bringing new ideas to the classroom and school; (d) polishing writing and presentation skills to share knowledge with others; (e) engaging in creative problem solving and decision making with increased student learning as the goal; (f) willingness to take risks in front of peers; and (g) willingness to share information, ideas, opinions, and evaluative judgments with the instructional leader with complete confidence.

Why Are Teacher Leaders Important?

> In an information-rich environment, no single individual is likely to have all the pieces of the puzzle needed to make sense of the situation.
>
> (Pajak, 1993, p. 178)

Effective instructional leaders recognize the importance of sharing the responsibility for developing the vision, making decisions, and implementing programs. In her study of excellent high schools, Lightfoot (1983) highlights this importance:

> In these good schools the image is one of teachers with voice and vision. Teachers are knowledgeable and discerning school actors who are the primary shapers of the educational environment. They are given a great deal of autonomy and authority in defining the intellectual agenda, but their individual quests are balanced against the requirement that they contribute to the broader school community. Most important, good schools are places that recognize the relationship between the learning and achievement of students and the development and expression of teachers. (p. 24)

Work constantly to help teachers develop and express themselves through collaborative and collegial relationships. Value and promote teachers working in teams, and willingly give responsibility for decision making to these teams. Little (1987) believes that the following benefits will return both to the school and the leader from this kind of encouragement: (a) teachers will complement each other's strengths and weaknesses thereby increasing total teaching effectiveness, (b) teachers will be more willing to take risks in their teaching, and (c) a culture of collaboration will induct new teachers more readily.

> Principals would do more lasting good for schools if they concentrated on building collaborative cultures rather than charging forcefully in with heavy agendas for change.
>
> (Fullan, 1992, p. 19)

Many instructional leaders have learned the hard way that failure to develop strong teacher leaders and share the yoke of leadership will result in one or more of these problems:

- You may miss the opportunity to learn from teachers and to grow as a professional.

- You may lose the power that shared leadership affords.

- You may win the battle but lose the war (i.e., think you are in charge but find out that you're really not).

- You may burn out from trying to do it all on your own.

Fullan and Hargreaves (1991) have summarized these pitfalls eloquently:

"My vision," "my teachers," "my school," are proprietary claims and attitudes which suggest an ownership of the school that is personal rather than collective, imposed rather than earned, and hierarchical rather than democratic. With visions as singular as this, teachers soon learn to suppress their voice. It does not get articulated. Management becomes manipulation. (p. 90)

Growing and Learning as a Professional

Making the fatal mistake of thinking you have all the answers and are the fount of all wisdom will, in effect, isolate you from any kind of personal or professional growth. Your staff will learn, in a dangerously fast fashion, that questioning the principal's judgment, sharing a radical idea, or pointing out that the emperor is indeed stark naked can all be suicidal acts. They will retreat to their classrooms and the teachers' lounge to grumble to each other. You will miss the opportunity, painful as it may often be, of learning from others.

> When a process makes people feel that they have a voice in matters that affect them, they will have a greater commitment to the overall enterprise and will take greater responsibility for what happens to the enterprise. The absence of such a process insures that no one feels responsible, that blame will always be directed externally, that adversarialism will be a notable feature of school life.
>
> (Sarason, 1990, p. 61)

Improving the Quality of Student Learning

Your focus as an instructional leader should always be student learning. The most powerful force for improving student learning is the collective energy, wisdom, and will of all the teachers in the learning community that is the school. Teachers who see principals as facilitators, supporters, and reinforcers for the jointly determined school mission rather than as guiders, directors, and leaders of their own personal agenda are far more likely to feel personally accountable for student learning. Sergiovanni (1992) believes that in the school communities of the future, "leadership will become less and less important, self-management will begin to take hold, and substitutes for leadership will become more deeply embedded in the school" (p. 42). I would beg to differ with Sergiovanni and want to revise his statement:

> In the school communities of the future, instructional leadership will be ever more challenging given the pressure for accountability on the one hand and the challenges of closing the achievement gaps in our country on the other. While self-management will increase, there will never be a substitute for a strong instructional leader. This individual, however, will need a cadre of strong teacher leaders to share the leadership load.

Winning the Battle but Losing the War

This is a metaphor for the classic mistake that many leaders make—leading the foot soldiers to a successful implementation in some minor skirmish while remaining totally oblivious to the havoc they have created with regard to troop morale or long-term deployment of resources. Many well-meaning instructional leaders have gone down in defeat, usually well documented historically and recounted for centuries, for lack of consulting, working with, and engaging all the junior officers.

Burnout

There is a real danger of growing disillusioned, disheartened, and discouraged if you do not have a group of energized, professional staff members surrounding you. Burnout is the all-too-common result of attempting to do everything on your own. The sense of isolation, frustration, and anger that often results from being the only cheerleader, resource provider, or idea person can demoralize even the most competent leader.

HOW CAN YOU DEVELOP TEACHER LEADERS?

The principal of a successful school is not the instructional leader but the coordinator of teachers as instructional leaders.

(Glickman, 1991, p. 7)

There are five primary ways that teachers can function as leaders in your school. They can

1. Train and provide staff development for other teachers

2. Coach and mentor other teachers

3. Develop and write curriculum

4. Be decision makers and leaders of school-making teams

5. Serve as members of teams, committees, task forces, or quality circles

An important prerequisite to the training and development of teacher leaders in any of these areas, however, must be the encouragement and fostering of a collegial atmosphere in your school. Without collegiality, teacher leaders will wither and die. Their efforts will be poorly received, your motivations as an instructional leader will be suspect, and everyone's time will be wasted. The journey from isolation to collegiality is often beset with obstacles and detours (Mahaffy, 1988), and there are several stopping-off points along the way: autocracy, coordination, accommodation, independence, cooperation, and collaboration (pp. 12-15).

At one end of the continuum is *autocracy*, a place of solitude where teachers work in isolation. "The autocratic teacher has no real colleagues and is a peer only in the sense there are often more such teachers in the school" (p. 12). *Coordination*, the second point on the continuum, is closely related to autocracy but goes beyond to include the fact that all the teachers in a school usually play by a common set of rules and agree on calendars, schedules, and other procedural matters. *Accommodation* is the next stopping-off place. Teachers in this phase use the same textbooks and curriculum and interact with their peers in a social way. *Independence*, the next point along the continuum, is seen by Mahaffy as "participatory interdependence." Teachers in this kind of school understand they are part of the larger school and its mission. They work alone but appreciate how what they do connects to others. *Cooperation*, the next resting place along the way, is characterized by teachers getting together to work for the accomplishment of a

DEVELOPING TEACHER LEADERS: SANDRA AHOLA, PRINCIPAL

Pomfret Community School, Pomfret, Connecticut

My favorite part of the principalship is playing to people's strengths. I do not believe in spending 90 percent of my time trying to fix, change, and improve 10 percent of my staff. Instead, I spend 90 percent of my time with 90 percent of my staff, and I feed the leaders. All principals know who these teachers are in their schools, and I personally encourage, enable, empower, provide funds for, release time for, and shower praise on them.

Finding each teacher's area of strength and building on it is the way to begin. In actuality, all teachers begin to excel and build on their own when they receive my unwavering support. I also make sure that my teachers are featured at board of education meetings. When I see a simple idea being carried out well by teachers who need a boost, I ask them to present their program at the next board of education meeting, which they always do with great success. I follow up the next morning with a brief announcement on the intercom and make sure that the whole staff knows once again that this person has excelled. Then I include a brief article in the school newsletter or the town paper to ensure that the whole world knows what a neat thing one of the Pomfret teachers did. I do not provide PR services, however, for those teachers who are not responding to my initiatives,

(continued)

Pomfret Community School
(continued)

my encouragement, and cues. I find that if you unleash the leaders in your school, feed them well in any way that you can (this means you need to know what it is that they value—praise, recognition, money, materials, release time to plan a new unit of study), then they will move the whole school. We all know that no one likes to be left behind, and that motivates even the most reluctant teachers to begin to move even a bit.

specific goal. Although they live in independence most of the time, when necessary, they can and do cooperate to accomplish a task. *Collaboration*, however, is the final and ultimate goal for any instructional leader—at the opposite end of autocracy. In collaboration, people work together, talk together, watch each other, help each other, and learn from each other. "The major difference [between collaboration and other states] is that in collaboration teachers and administrators share a common paradigm—a philosophy that guides their decisions and their professionalism" (p. 15).

Teachers as Trainers

The belief that consultants and experts can always do a more effective job as trainers and staff developers can stand in the way of developing teacher leaders. Give your teachers the same kind of professional courtesies and respect you pay a visiting consultant. Pay them for their preparation time. Require that participants sign up in advance for the privilege of hearing them speak. Provide appropriate facilities and equipment to make the presentation more professional. And give your teachers helpful feedback and evaluation so they will continue to improve and grow. Each and every time teachers prepare a workshop or presentation for another group of teachers, their own teaching performance and effectiveness improves. In my opinion, staff development dollars spent on teachers training teachers will double your investment.

> [The term] instructional leader suggests that others have got to be followers. The legitimate instructional leaders, if we have to have them, ought to be teachers. And principals ought to be leaders of leaders: people who develop the instructional leadership in their teachers.
>
> (Sergiovanni, 1992, p. 48)

Convincing the powers that be that teachers are professionals who learn best from one another is the central issue. In the financial crunch facing so many school districts it would seem easier to "sell" a program that does not require high priced consultants, expensive materials, and disruption of classes than the more typical inservice experience that often requires all three. Strange as it seems, districts will often pay the price for the legitimacy of the expensive "expert" rather than put those resources into using their own staffs as experts. (Roper & Hoffman, 1986, p. 24)

Teachers as Curriculum Writers and Authors

Don't make the mistake of thinking that your teachers can't develop curriculum that will measure up to the highest standards. Send them to workshops; give them time to study and plan together; and bring in consultants to advise when necessary. But then, just let them create. It won't be perfect in the beginning, but the process is infinitely more important than the product. And the products will begin to improve with practice.

Teachers as Decision Makers

If you haven't discovered the power of sharing the leadership of your school with a team of teachers, you've missed one of the most powerful, growth-evoking experiences available to a building principal. Rather than weakening your power base or making you less effective as an instructional leader, sharing leadership will increase your influence. Garfield (1986) pointed out in his study of peak performers that leaders who develop, reward, and recognize those around them are "simply allowing the human assets with which they work to appreciate in value" (p. 182). The schools in West Chicago, Illinois, have employed site-based management and building leadership teams in their schools since 1985. A team of four teachers (each serving a 2-year term) meets monthly for a half day of release time to solve problems, set goals, design programs, and focus on student learning. The unique populations and challenges of each school result in different agendas for each team, but the overall focus must always relate to the overall district goal of learning for all.

> You can't mandate what matters.
> (Fullan, 1997, p. 15)

Using the team approach to change has many advantages. Teams can

- Set priorities so that too much change is not dumped on the school with no sense of what is most important
- Model the kinds of behavior that they would like to elicit from colleagues
- Anticipate objections so that the answers are provided before some of the negative reactions are registered (Maeroff, 1993, p. 515)

Teachers as Members of Committees, Task Forces, and Teams

Phyllis O'Connell develops teacher leaders when she asks for volunteers to study new issues, become specialists in new curricular areas, or train other staff members in new techniques. These small groups meet on their own with a chairperson and report back to the faculty or building leadership team as necessary. When Phyllis senses that the school should be moving in a new direction, she strategizes ways in which her faculty can study and learn about the issue on their own before discussing it as a possible direction in which to go. Teachers, rather than the principal, become the chief spokespersons for change. Teams can also be formed as part of the instructional delivery system (grade-level, departmental, and interdisciplinary). Or they can be formed on an ad hoc basis to solve disciplinary problems, develop new recognition programs, or assist in selecting new staff members. This approach is widely used in the business world. "Whether called task forces, quality circles, problem solving groups, or shared responsibility teams, such vehicles for greater participation are an important part of an innovating company" (Kanter, 1983, p. 241). They are a necessity for the improving school and the effective instructional leader.

TEACHERS AS COLLABORATORS: KATHIE DOBBERTEEN, PRINCIPAL

La Mesa Dale Elementary School, La Mesa, California

Five years ago, staff meetings were conducted each week to disseminate information and discuss some schoolwide issues. In the past 5 years, an evolution has taken place, and now teachers meet in grade level teams at least twice per month. They work on long- and short-term plans, analyze student work, discuss methods for reaching standards, and so forth. The teaching staff has developed a strong spirit of collegiality and is committed to bringing its best to students. Over time, the unifying focus of leaving no child behind has created an underlying desire to constantly refine and improve our instructional delivery. (Dobberteen, 2001, p. 4)

Teachers as Researchers

Lieberman (1988) believes that involving teachers in doing research can develop leadership skills and result in powerful professional development. She suggests three areas for potential interactive research: (a) curricular concerns (How do students learn math concepts best?), (b) instructional concerns (How can time-on-task be increased in my classroom?), and (c) overall professional concerns (What are the factors that contribute to high morale in a school?).

HOW CAN YOU KEEP YOUR TEAM FOCUSED?

This is critically important. Anyone who has participated in a leadership team will concur with the following observation made by a teacher team member: "You get bogged down in micromanagement: The bathrooms are dirty, the lights are out somewhere, and the intercom doesn't work" (Bradley & Olson, 1993, p. 11). The focus of the team should be student learning and achievement. Keeping that focus is the key role of the instructional leader. Establish guidelines about the types of issues that your team will discuss, the length of time you'll devote to noninstructional issues, and how skillfully to redirect team members who veer off task.

HOW CAN YOU BUILD CONSENSUS?

Trust and mutual respect are the key elements to successful group decision making and consensus building. The effective instructional leaders use a variety of techniques, for even when a finely tuned school leadership team comes up with an outstanding recommendation, that group still needs to gain the approval and support of the faculty at large.

Dave Burton avoids building consensus on important issues in a large group setting such as a faculty meeting. Instead, he works through his leadership team members or through the team leaders in his middle school. They are individuals in whom he has a great deal of confidence, and he trusts them to communicate effectively with the people they represent. When he feels he has an especially touchy issue on the agenda, he finds that pizza and soft drinks have a soothing effect on his staff.

Other instructional leaders hold multiple informal discussions. Linda Hanson works constantly—small groups, ad hoc groups, large groups, writing to staff, focus groups, debates. She says, "Everything is done through mutual respect." Chris Gaylord keeps bringing up agenda items until her faculty has really worked through them. She doesn't rush and waits until teachers have ownership in both the problem and the solutions. Nick Friend goes out and sells his ideas at times. He calls it "gentle, relentless pressure." Some instructional leaders still have difficulty with this skill, particularly if they believe strongly about issues and think that students are suffering. They are impatient for things to happen. They feel frustration at the shortsightedness of some faculty. "Consensus does not happen as quickly as I would like. I feel that we will never agree on some issues of education. This is hard!" says Alan Jones. But they are learning to take the necessary steps. He says,

> I'm in the process of making a cognitive shift in this area. In order to reach consensus, you must be willing to share information and responsibility. In addition, you should possess communication skills that allow a group to get to a "third alternative."

The culture of the school must reflect a belief that everyone's ideas are important and will be considered. Effective instructional leaders are never reluctant to back off if the entire staff (or a good portion of it) are not willing to move forward on a particular plan or idea. They recognize the importance of listening to the professional staff. The idea may be a good one that needs more time to gel. The idea may be a bad one that has been sold by a terrific sales presentation. Or the faculty may have too many other priorities at the time. There are many valid reasons for tabling an issue.

> The empowerment of teachers and strong instructional leadership on the part of the principal are not mutually exclusive. Principals who empower their staffs do not simply turn teachers loose, let them go off and do whatever they want and hope for the best.
>
> (DuFour, 1991, pp. 33-34)

High school administrator Angie Garcia (1986) has summarized a list of particularly helpful guidelines for reaching consensus. But don't assume that everyone will automatically understand and subscribe to these guidelines. Effective instructional leaders spend time training and working with teacher leaders to develop common understandings as well as skills to implement these principles:

• Avoid arguing for your own individual judgments. Present your positions as clearly as possible, but listen to other members' reactions and consider the logic before pressing your point.

• Do not assume that someone must win and someone must lose when discussion reaches a stalemate. Instead, look for the next most acceptable alternative for all.

• Keep the discussion focused on what you can agree on, even if it is only one small point.

• Do not change your mind simply to avoid conflict. Be suspicious when agreement comes too quickly and easily.

• Avoid conflict-reducing techniques such as majority vote, averaging coin flips, and bargaining. When a dissenting member finally agrees, don't feel that person must be rewarded later.

• Differences of opinion are natural and expected. Disagreements can help the group decision because with a wide range of information, there is a greater chance that the group will hit on more adequate solutions.

• When you can't seem to get anywhere in a large group, break into smaller groups and try to reach consensus. Then return to the larger group and try again.

• When one or two members simply can't agree with the group after a reasonable period of time, ask them to deliver a minority report based on their logic.

There are three ways to enhance consensus building: (a) Give people time to build relationships; (b) deal only with important and meaningful issues; and (c) give teachers support and affirmation for their efforts.

Give People Time to Build Relationships

Teachers need time if you really want to foster a supportive environment that develops teacher leaders and encourages collaborative planning. They need time in other locations (restaurants, conference centers, people's homes); they need time to work with people from other grade levels and disciplines and from the same grade levels and disciplines; they need time to solve specific problems; they need time to plan for the future; they need planning meetings at the beginning of the school year; and they need evaluative meetings at the end of the school year.

Work With Important Issues

Never waste teachers' time on issues they (the majority of the group) don't care about. You will lose credibility and, more important, you will waste valuable time. Time is a precious commodity and not to be squandered on issues like lights for the parking lot or which fundraiser to use. Let the people who care about those issues make the decisions. Your time should be devoted to issues of teaching and learning.

Give Teachers Support and Affirmation for Their Decisions

In the words of one veteran teacher, "Don't ask for my opinion if you aren't prepared to live with the consequences." If you're not willing and able to support the changes that teachers recommend, then don't even begin to encourage participatory decision making or develop teacher leaders on your faculty.

HOW CAN YOU MAXIMIZE YOUR TIME WITH STAFF?

There's a well-worn phrase used to describe the time that parents and children spend together—quality time. This same phrase can be used to describe the kind of time you and your staff members spend together. You can maximize that time by planning and conducting good meetings— faculty meetings, planning meetings, team meetings, grade-level meetings, problem-solving meetings. You will need the ability to lead, follow, listen, summarize, brainstorm, organize, manage conflict, and know when to adjourn.

The instructional leaders we interviewed had these helpful suggestions for planning and organizing effective meetings:

- Provide printed agendas at least two days in advance (if appropriate for the nature of the meeting).

- Test the water ahead of time for input.

- Staff members must laugh together before working together.

- Appoint someone different at each meeting to graphically chart the proceedings of the meeting so that everyone can see what is being recorded. Use lots of different-colored markers, illustrations, and flow charts to make the meeting come alive on paper. This will help to summarize the meeting in a written form later. Make sure any decisions reached at the meeting are disseminated as quickly as possible in the days that follow the meeting.

- Expect and reinforce professional behavior. Don't talk when others are talking. Respect other people's ideas and opinions. Be positive.

- Organize in small discussion groups and then culminate with a full faculty meeting.

- Set a beginning and ending time and never start (even if everyone's not there) or end late.

- Never make or read announcements that staff members can read themselves.

- The principal should be the organizer, not the orator.

- Serve food when appropriate.

- Get everyone involved. Don't allow one or two individuals to monopolize the meeting.

- Give staff members a writing activity at the end of the meeting to focus their thinking and planning.

- If consensus isn't occurring, postpone the decision. Few decisions *must* be made today.

- Make certain that the discussion is moving forward and not in circles.

- Share accomplishments.

- Always end on a positive note.

- Praise, praise, praise!

HOW CAN YOU USE THE INSTRUCTIONAL LEADERSHIP CHECKLIST TO ASSESS STEP SIX?

Step Six: Develop Teacher Leaders

There are three indicators that describe this step in more detail. Each indicator is followed by three sections: (a) a *comment* that defines the specific focus of the indicator; (b) a *scale of descriptors* that gives a continuum of behaviors (1 to 5) from least effective to most effective; and (c) *key points in the descriptors* that give succinct explanations of each of the five items in the scale. For each indicator, select the number from 1 to 5 that most accurately describes your own behavior on a day-to-day basis.

> **MUST-READ BOOKS TO ASSIST YOU IN IMPLEMENTING STEP SIX**
>
> Jo Blase & Joseph Blase. (1998). *Handbook of Instructional Leadership.* Thousand Oaks, CA: Corwin.
> J. Blase & P. C. Kirby. (2000). *Bringing Out the Best in Teachers.* Thousand Oaks, CA: Corwin.
> L. Bolman & T. Deal. (1994). *Becoming a Teacher Leader: From Isolation to Collaboration.* Thousand Oaks, CA: Corwin.
> E. K. McEwan. (1997). *Leading Your Team to Excellence: How to Make Quality Decisions.* Thousand Oaks, CA: Corwin.
> E. K. McEwan. (2001). *Ten Traits of Highly Effective Teachers: How to Hire, Mentor, and Coach Successful Teachers.* Thousand Oaks, CA: Corwin.

Indicator 6.1

Schedules, plans, or facilitates regular meetings of all types (planning, problem solving, decision making, or inservice and training) with and among teachers to address instructional issues.

Comment

The main focus of Indicator 6.1 is both the quantity and quality of meetings that discuss instructional issues.

Scale of Descriptors

1. Few meetings are held, instructional issues are never discussed, and no shared decision making or collaboration is evident.

2. Meetings are held on an as-needed basis, instructional issues are rarely discussed, and no shared decision making or collaboration is evident.

3. Meetings are regularly scheduled, instructional issues are sometimes discussed, and some shared decision making or collaboration is evident.

4. Meetings are regularly scheduled, instructional issues are discussed on an as-needed basis, and some shared decision making and collaboration are evident.

5. Meetings of all types are regularly scheduled, and instructional issues are discussed on a continuing basis. Shared decision making and collaboration characterize all meetings.

Key Points in Descriptors

1. Few meetings held. No instructional discussions. No shared decision making or collaboration.

2. Few meetings held. Rare instructional discussions. No shared decision making collaboration.

3. Regularly scheduled meetings. Some instructional discussions. Some shared decision making and collaboration.

4. Regularly scheduled meetings. Regularly scheduled instructional discussions. Some shared decision making and collaboration.

5. Regularly scheduled meetings with continuing discussion of instructional issues.

Indicator 6.2

Provides opportunities for, and training in, collaboration, shared decision making, coaching, mentoring, curriculum development, and presentations.

Comment

The main focus of Indicator 6.2 is the provision of opportunities, as well as provision of training, in all areas of teacher leadership.

Scale of Descriptors

1. Principal never provides opportunities or training for teachers to develop leadership skills.

2. Principal provides some opportunities and training for teachers to develop leadership skills but does so in a highly controlled and regulated fashion.

3. Principal provides some opportunities and training for teachers to develop leadership skills but permits a great deal of latitude in the exercise of these skills and does not use them or focus them in an organized way.

4. Principal provides multiple opportunities and training for teachers to develop leadership skills and uses these skills to improve

instruction, coordinate with building the mission, and improve student learning.

5.   Principal provides multiple opportunities and training for teachers to develop leadership skills, uses them to continually improve instruction in classrooms, and has a school leadership team that participates in the continual improvement of the school.

Key Points in Descriptors

1. No opportunities or training.

2. Some opportunities and training but not relevant to needs.

3. Opportunities and training provided that are relevant to faculty needs.

4. Opportunities and training provided that are relevant to faculty needs and relate to improvement of instruction.

5. Opportunities and training provided that are relevant to faculty needs; relate to improvement of instruction; are jointly planned, evaluated, and followed up; and include a systematic school improvement process under the leadership of a school team.

Indicator 6.3

Provides motivation and resources for faculty members to engage in professional-growth activities.

Comment

The focus of Indicator 6.3 is the encouragement provided by the principal to faculty members either by personal example or positive reinforcement as well as the allocation of available resources to support professional-growth activities.

Scale of Descriptors

1.   Principal never engages in personal professional-growth activities and discourages teachers from doing so by failing to allocate resources for this activity in the budget.

2.   Principal never engages in personal professional-growth activities and although monies are available for teacher activities, does not motivate or positively reinforce those teachers who do so.

3.   Principal engages in personal professional-growth activities and allocates resources for teachers to do so as well, but does not motivate or positively reinforce those teachers who do so.

4.   Principal engages in personal professional-growth activities, allocates resources for teachers to do so as well, and motivates and positively reinforces those teachers who do so.

5.   Principal engages in personal professional-growth activities, allocates available resources for teachers to do so as well, motivates teachers to engage in activities that will benefit the building's instructional program, and uses expertise in sharing with other teachers.

Key Points in Descriptors

1. No personal professional-growth activities; no motivation or reinforcement; no resources for teachers.

2. No personal professional-growth activities; no motivation or reinforcement; some allocation of resources.

3. Personal professional-growth activities; allocation of resources; no motivation or reinforcement.

4. Personal professional-growth activities; allocation of available resources, motivation, and reinforcement.

5. Personal professional-growth activities; allocation of resources, motivation, and reinforcement; use of teachers in building activities.

Step Seven: Establish and Maintain Positive Relationships With Students, Staff, and Parents

Autry (1991) said, "Good management is largely a matter of love. Or if you are uncomfortable with that word, call it caring" (p. 13). The Apostle Paul put it this way: "If I had the gift of being able to speak in tongues, and could speak in every language there is in all of heaven and earth, but I didn't love others, it would be of no value whatever. I would only be making a lot of noise" (*The Living Bible*, 1971, p. 1160). Covey (1989) calls it seeking first to understand rather than to be understood. Autry, the Apostle Paul, and Covey have all discovered and articulated a principle that effective instructional leaders seek to practice in their daily lives—attitudes and relationships are the keys to being effective.

The leadership literature is replete with examples of individuals who have the necessary competence to do the job—they just don't have people skills. There are many well-meaning administrators who have all the necessary certification, know good instruction, and even

> Anybody could lead perfect people—if there were any. But there aren't any perfect people. . . . People grow taller when those who lead them empathize and when they are accepted for what they are, even though their performance may be judged critically in terms of what they are capable of doing.
>
> (Greenleaf, 1977, p. 21)

have a vision of what their school could and should become. But they are remarkably like Ed, a CEO described by Bennis (1989):

> He was very competent and very ambitious, but he was also a tyrant. He was impulsive and frequently abusive of people who worked for him. They would actually cower in his presence. He had a desperate need to control both people and events. He was incapable of thanking anyone for a job well done—he couldn't even give a compliment. (p. 26)

Fostering and maintaining positive relationships with students, staff, and parents are critical to effectiveness as an instructional leader. Here, two principals reflect on their work:

> I want to be viewed as a person who listens and cares for each person as an individual. I shake hands with children, bus drivers, moms, dads, grandparents, and neighbors, and I pet the dogs. I have strong opinions about education and life, but I try to treat all people who enter the building as customers. I enjoy my profession and it shows.

> I believe that I can work with just about any type of individual. I don't expect perfection from anyone, but I do expect hard work, a sincere interest in children, and dedication. I have the ability to listen. I listen to angry parents, and hurt teachers, but it's very rare that they leave angry or hurt.

HOW CAN YOU SERVE AS AN ADVOCATE FOR STUDENTS?

The instructional leaders I interviewed view student advocacy as a part of their overall vision and mission. "The whole point of everything we do is for students," said Linda Hanson. Frances Starks adds, "Students are the reason we have our jobs, and we owe them the best of what we have to give. Their concern and development come first."

Effective instructional leaders don't just talk about how much they care about students. They show how much they care by their actions. On a daily basis, they work to change inequitable policies and practices in the areas of discipline, grading, and grouping; they volunteer in a variety of community activities; they develop close personal relationships with students; and their doors are always open to troubled students.

Discipline

While effective instructional leaders believe in the importance of discipline and are firm and fair disciplinarians, they also recognize that the system doesn't always work for students. Carol Auer often pleads that students be given the benefit of the doubt and frequently enlightens teachers about a situation that may change their views of a child's behavior. Alan Jones is similarly motivated:

I investigate all student complaints about teachers or implementation of policies. I will intervene aggressively, if I feel a student has been wronged. You really walk a tightrope in this area. Teachers are sensitive to the support issue. But I think you must send a message that students are people and deserve an audience.

Grading Practices

Effective instructional leaders also intervene as a student advocate when grading practices seem unfair. "All of us have tunnel vision about our jobs," Brent McArdle believes. "Bringing a student perspective to something like grading practices sometimes helps a teacher from becoming too myopic."

ACKNOWLEDGING THE MEANINGFUL ACCOMPLISHMENTS OF OTHERS: KATHIE DOBBERTEEN, PRINCIPAL

La Mesa Dale Elementary School, La Mesa, California

We recognize staff members regularly for their outstanding efforts in working with students that result in significant academic growth. Teachers receive individual notes of appreciation. Their successes are noted in writing when analyses of their assessment results are distributed. Each year, for the past 5 years, we have celebrated our exceptional half-year student growth in reading with a party at a midyear staff meeting. One year, we celebrated with cake and sparkling cider. Last year's celebration of success took the form of a Hugs and Kisses party. This year we applauded Stellar Student Achievement with certificates and refreshments. Paper stars were spread on every conceivable surface in the meeting room, including the floor. Staff members know that they are extremely successful in reaching their students, but they enjoy these celebrations immensely. (Dobberteen, 2000, p. 13)

Community

Student advocacy is not limited to the hours that school is in session. For some instructional leaders, their commitment to students extends nearly 24 hours a day. Mike Pettibone is involved in Little League, Saturday intramurals, Saturday enrichments, Friday Night Prime Times, and even serves as a reading buddy at the public library.

Instructional Issues

It is in the area of opportunities for learning that instructional leaders are the most eloquent advocates for students. "I am constantly striving for quality instructional time, attention to individual differences, and programs that allow the active participation of all children regardless of ability," says Richard Seyler. Bob Hassan knows each and every student their strengths, weaknesses, and needs. He is intimately involved in all program reviews, placement decisions, and academic conferences.

Schools are not buildings, curriculum, and machines. Schools are relationships and interactions among people.

(Johnson & Johnson, 1989, p. 1)

While large meetings and grand symbolic actions play a part, the most significant change in work culture is accomplished in one-to-one personal interactions.

(Sagor, 1992, p. 18)

Counselor, Listener, and Friend

Effective instructional leaders care about students. Nick and Mary Ann Friend both have wonderful personal relationships with their students. Their students are keenly aware that the Friends are really true friends. They attend activities, show affection, and acknowledge their successes. They take students to lunch and send personal cards and notes.

Students are willing to confide in Dave Burton. "Based on the number of students who come to me with problems or just to talk, I feel that they trust me. They know that my primary purpose is to work with them, and they know that my door is always open to them."

WHAT ARE THE KEY HUMAN RELATIONS SKILLS?

Effective instructional leaders are confident about their abilities to get along with just about anyone. They are able to articulate what they do well and are always willing to learn. Nancy Carbone summarized it this way:

I think the main human relations skill I possess is the willingness to give people a voice in the daily business of the school. I firmly believe that inviting people to participate in decision making is what makes a school work best. I am also willing to admit when I am wrong and to change a course of action if most of the staff members feel it is not advisable for the school.

Instructional leaders are unanimous in selecting the one skill they believe is essential—listening. And they highlight these aspects of effective listening as particularly important:

- Make eye contact.
- Give your undivided attention.
- Send nonverbal signals that you are interested and that you care; for example, don't shuffle papers or keep on writing when someone is with you or comes to the door.
- Be able to restate or rephrase what is being said when appropriate.
- Don't interrupt. Instructional leaders are constantly being interrupted, but you must guard against sending the message to teachers or parents that you don't have time to talk.

In addition to the skill of listening, countless other human relations skills are also important. They were each cited by many of the interviewed instructional leaders:

- Be willing to admit when you're wrong.
- Be able to laugh (have a good sense of humor) and cry (display sensitivity and empathy).
- Take time to help others.
- Remember how it felt to be a child.
- Be able to resolve conflicts between people.
- Be able to remain calm in stressful situations.
- Enjoy working with people of all ages.
- Truly care about others.
- Realize that you can't please everyone.
- Be optimistic about people's motives.

HOW CAN YOU DEVELOP MORALE?

Morale is a mental condition with respect to several characteristics, among them confidence and enthusiasm (McKechnie, 1983, p. 1168). Morale in a school setting is an integral part of the culture of the school—the feelings you get when you walk in the building, how people treat each other, how they feel about their work, and

> Listening to your school helps you succeed in two basic ways: it tells you where and how your leadership is needed, and it tells you how you are doing as a leader. Think of the school as your teacher.
>
> (Ackerman, Donaldson, & van der Bogert, 1996, p. 159)

how they talk about what they do. When morale is poor, there is a sense of powerlessness on the part of people. Teachers feel powerless to impact students. Students feel like pawns and puppets whose only recourse is to revolt.

And parents feel manipulated and used. Many effective instructional leaders have been hired into settings just like that. What have they done to build morale? Simple things like sending out a questionnaire and then listening carefully to people's responses. Superintendent Linda Murphy of Kenilworth, Illinois, has served as a principal in several schools and districts. An avid learner and practitioner of the school culture literature, her first act on assuming a new principalship is to ask the following important questions of all staff members. She may do this in a written questionnaire, small focus discussion groups, or in individual conferences:

- As your new building principal, how can I best support you during this school year?
- What are this school's most recent successes?
- How do you think this school ought to change?
- What is one thing that you are most excited about this year?
- What do you like most and least about working at this school?
- What causes you the greatest stress in your work?
- What is important to the parents of this school?
- What are our students like?
- What format for decision making would you recommend at the building level?
- What curriculum issues need attention at this school?
- What are your overall impressions of this school—its strengths and weaknesses?
- What is the key issue that this school faces in the near future? What should I know about this issue? How should it be resolved?
- How are important decisions made relative to this school? How effective is this process? Should it be changed? If so, how?
- What are you proudest of relative to this school? What is your proudest accomplishment while working here?
- What would you like me to know that I have not asked?

With the answers to these questions in hand, Murphy has a clear picture of the morale in her new school. She also has a ready-made list of priorities for morale building (if needed) and knows exactly where to begin working with teachers, parents, and students.

HOW CAN YOU ACKNOWLEDGE THE ACHIEVEMENTS OF OTHERS?

Acknowledging the meaningful accomplishments of others is part of morale building, but it must happen in an atmosphere of honesty, collegiality, and caring. There is nothing more devastating to morale than phony praise calculated to accomplish hidden agendas. Praise and celebration must be grounded in the mission of the school, embedded in the culture of the community, and sincerely given in the spirit of appreciation and caring. The recognition of accomplishments must be shared by all and appreciated by all.

Here are some ways that outstanding instructional leaders acknowledge the accomplishments of students, teachers, and parents.

Celebrate Success

Kindergarten through sixth-grade students are recognized monthly for outstanding Academics, Behavior, or Citizenship (ABC) at the Allenwood School in Allenwood, New Jersey. Principal Harry Baldwin structures the ABC assemblies to include parents, applause, handshaking, and lots of photo opportunities for each student. Group photos are taken by grade level and displayed all year on the ABC recognition board in a large common area.

> Nothing motivates a child more than when learning is valued by school, family, and community working in partnership.
>
> (Fullan, 1997, p. 22)

Golden Apple Awards

Ann Parker, elementary principal in Canton, Missouri, presents Golden Apple awards to staff members and homerooms that have made a noteworthy contribution to improving the school climate. The recipients are presented with a small brass apple that remains with them for the week. Then the apple is passed on to the next Golden Apple winner.

MUST-READ BOOKS TO ASSIST YOU IN IMPLEMENTING STEP SEVEN

J. R. Hoyle. (2001). *Leadership and the Force of Love: Six Keys to Motivating With Love.* Thousand Oaks, CA: Corwin.

J. A. Kottler & E. K. McEwan. (1999). *Counseling Tips for Elementary School Principals.* Thousand Oaks, CA: Corwin.

E. K. McEwan. (1998). *How to Deal with Parents Who Are Angry, Troubled, Afraid, or Just Plain Crazy.* Thousand Oaks, CA: Corwin.

Parent Hall of Fame

In an effort to make the school a welcome place for parents, a prominent area in the lobby of the school has been designated as the Parent Hall of Fame in Nancy Carbone's school in Greenwich, Connecticut. Each month, individual parents or groups of parents are nominated to be honored. The school media specialist photographs the individuals and creates an attractive, ongoing display.

Get It While It's Hot

Joyce Roberts of Farmington, New Mexico, carries a small tape recorder with her as she walks through the halls to record student work displays. On returning to her office, she hands the tape to her secretary who makes certificates to give to staff and students who are deserving of special recognition.

Congratulations

At the end of each semester, the president of the local bank in Boaz, Alabama, sends letters of congratulations to honor roll students at Amelia Cartrett's school. The bank has adopted the school, and the letters are just another way of recognizing the achievements of students.

Crackerjack Job

When a faculty or staff member does an exceptional job or gives that extra effort for a project or activity, Danny Shaw at the Calhoun Elementary School in Anderson, South Carolina, acknowledges them with a personal thank-you note and a box of Cracker Jacks.

On-the-Spot Bonuses

Increasingly, on-the-spot bonuses are being adopted by high-tech companies as a way to motivate with the power of instant gratification. (Popcorn & Hanft, 2001, p. 77). With a little creativity and the help of some teachers, come up with a list of on-the-spot bonuses that you can award to star teachers and students as you notice outstanding achievement.

HOW CAN YOU USE THE INSTRUCTIONAL LEADERSHIP CHECKLIST TO ASSESS STEP SEVEN?

Step Seven: Establish and Maintain Positive Relationships With Students, Staff, and Parents

There are seven indicators that describe this step in more detail. Each indicator is followed by three sections: (a) a *comment* that defines the specific focus of the indicator; (b) a *scale of descriptors* that gives a continuum of behaviors (1 to 5) from least effective to most effective; and (c) *key points in the descriptors* that give succinct explanations of each of the five items in the scale. For each indicator, select the number from 1 to 5 that most accurately describes your own behavior on a day-to-day basis.

Indicator 7.1

Serves as an advocate for students and communicates with them regarding their school life.

Comment

The main focus of Indicator 7.1 is the behaviors that the principal exhibits that give evidence of student advocacy and interaction with students. Behaviors might include lunch with individual students or groups; frequent appearances on the playground, in the lunchroom, and in the hallways; sponsorship of clubs; availability to students who wish to discuss instructional or disciplinary concerns; knowledge of students' names and family relationships; addressing the majority of students by name; and willingness to listen to the students' side in a faculty-student problem. The preceding list is *only* meant to be suggestive of the types of behaviors that might be appropriate for consideration in this category.

Scale of Descriptors

1. Principal does not feel that acting as a student advocate is an appropriate role of the principal and never interacts with students.

2. Principal does not feel that acting as a student advocate is an appropriate role of the principal and seldom interacts with students.

3. Principal does not feel that acting as a student advocate is an appropriate role of the principal but regularly engages in at least three behaviors that encourage communication between student and principal.

4. Principal feels that acting as a student advocate is an appropriate role of the principal and regularly engages in at least six behaviors that encourage communication between student and principal.

5. Principal feels that acting as a student advocate is an appropriate role of the principal, regularly engages in at least six behaviors that encourage communication between student and principal, and has established some means of receiving input from students regarding their opinions of school life.

Key Points in Descriptors

1. No role as an advocate; no interaction with students.

2. No role as an advocate; rare interaction with students.

3. No role as an advocate; three behaviors that encourage communication.

4. Role as student advocate; six behaviors that encourage communication.

5. Role as an advocate; six behaviors that encourage communication; some means of receiving student input.

Indicator 7.2

Encourages open communication among staff members and maintains respect for differences of opinion.

Comment

The main focus of Indicator 7.2 is the behaviors the principal exhibits that give evidence of maintenance of open communication among staff members and respect for differences of opinion. Behaviors might include open-door policy in the principal's office, acceptance of unpopular ideas and negative feedback from faculty, provision of channels for faculty members to voice grievances or discuss problems, or provision of channels for faculty members to discuss their work with each other. The preceding list is *only* meant to be suggestive of the types of behaviors that might be appropriate for consideration in this category.

Scale of Descriptors

1. Principal does not encourage open communication among staff members and considers differences of opinion to be a sign of disharmony among organizational members.

2. Principal supports open communication but is seldom available for informal encounters with staff members. Appointments must be scheduled, meeting agendas are tightly maintained, and the flow of information and opinions is artificially controlled.

3. Principal supports open communication and is available for informal encounters with staff members. Principal is not responsive, however, to problems, questions, or disagreements and shuts off communication of this nature.

4. Principal supports open communication and is available for informal encounters with staff members. Principal is responsive to problems, questions, or disagreements and encourages staff members to work through differences of opinion in positive ways.

5. Principal supports open communication and is available for informal encounters with staff members. An open-door policy exists with

regard to all problems, questions, and disagreements. Principal structures a variety of opportunities for faculty members to interact both formally and informally, encouraging interaction between grade levels, departments, and instructional teams.

Key Points in Descriptors

1. Discourages open communication.

2. Exhibits few behaviors that encourage open communication.

3. Exhibits some behaviors that encourage open communication.

4. Exhibits many behaviors that encourage open communication and facilitates problem solving among staff members.

5. Exhibits many behaviors that encourage open communication; facilitates problem solving among staff members; and structures many opportunities for staff interaction.

Indicator 7.3

Demonstrates concern and openness in the consideration of teacher, parent, and student problems and participates in the resolution of such problems where appropriate.

Comment

The main focus of Indicator 7.3 is the behaviors the principal exhibits in the consideration and resolution of problems.

Scale of Descriptors

1. Principal does not wish to be involved in the consideration of teacher, parent, and student problems.

2. Principal is willing to be involved in the consideration of teacher, parent, and student problems but is largely ineffective because of poor communication and human relations skills.

3. Principal is willing to be involved in the consideration of teacher, parent, and student problems and is sometimes effective in bringing problems to resolution. Exhibits average communication and human relations skills.

4. Principal is willing to be involved in the consideration of teacher, parent, and student problems and is usually effective in bringing problems

to resolution. Exhibits excellent communication and human relations skills.

5. Principal is willing to be involved in the consideration of teacher, parent, and student problems and is nearly always effective in bringing problems to resolution. Exhibits outstanding communication and human relations skills. Has established procedures jointly with faculty for the resolution of problems.

Key Points in Descriptors

1. No involvement.

2. Some involvement; ineffective problem-solver.

3. Involvement; average problem-solving skills.

4. Involvement; excellent problem-solving skills.

5. Involvement; outstanding problem-solving skills.

Indicator 7.4

Models appropriate human relations skills.

Comment

The main focus of Indicator 7.4 is the variety of appropriate human relations skills that are exhibited by the principal. Behaviors *must* include, but not necessarily be limited to, establishing a climate of trust and security for students and staff; respecting the rights of students, parents, and staff; handling individual relationships tactfully and with understanding; and accepting the dignity and worth of individuals without regard to appearance, race, creed, sex, disability, ability, or social status.

Scale of Descriptors

1. Principal has almost no human relations skills.

2. Principal has marginal human relations skills.

3. Principal has average human relations skills.

4. Principal has excellent human relations skills.

5. Principal has outstanding human relations skills.

Key Points in Descriptors

1. Principal exhibits none of the behaviors listed for this indicator under Comment.

2. Principal exhibits only one or two behaviors listed for this indicator under Comment and often has difficulty with tasks that involve human interaction.

3. Principal exhibits two or three of the behaviors listed for this indicator under Comment and is usually successful with tasks that involve human interaction.

4. Principal exhibits three or four of the behaviors listed for this indicator under Comment and is frequently successful with tasks that involve human interaction.

5. Principal exhibits all of the behaviors listed for this indicator under Comment as well as many other behaviors associated with good human relations and is almost always successful with tasks that involve human interaction.

Indicator 7.5

Develops and maintains high morale.

Comment

The main focus of Indicator 7.5 is the variety of behaviors exhibited by the principal that contribute to the development and maintenance of high morale. Behaviors might include, but not necessarily be limited to, involvement of staff in planning, encouragement of planned social events, openness in the dissemination of information, equity in the division of responsibility and allocation of resources, opportunities for achievement, recognition for achievements, involvement of the staff in problem solving, and assistance and support with personal and professional problems.

Scale of Descriptors

1. Morale is nonexistent in the school building. Principal exhibits none of the behaviors listed in the Comment section for this indicator. There is little unity among staff members, leading to competition, clique formation, destructive criticism, disagreement, and quarreling.

2. Morale is marginal in the school building. Principal exhibits few of the behaviors listed in the Comment section for this indicator. Although fewer visible signs of disunity are evident, faculty members, nevertheless, do not work well together or have positive feelings about their work.

3. Morale is average. Although there are no visible signs of disunity (such as those listed in Descriptor 1 of this scale), teachers work largely as

individuals, seldom working together cooperatively with enthusiasm and positive feelings.

4. Morale is excellent. Morale-building behaviors by the principal result in teachers working together to share ideas and resources, to identify instructional problems, to define mutual goals, and to coordinate their activities.

5. Morale is outstanding. Morale-building behaviors by the principal result in teachers working together in a highly effective way while gaining personal satisfaction from their work. Principal has identified specific activities that build morale and systematically engages in these activities.

Key Points in Descriptors

1. Nonexistent morale

2. Marginal morale

3. Average morale

4. Excellent morale

5. Outstanding morale

Indicator 7.6

Systematically collects and responds to staff, parent, and student concerns.

Comment

The main focus of Indicator 7.6 is the responsiveness of the principal to the concerns of staff, parents, and students that have been systematically collected. Examples of vehicles used to collect information might include, but not necessarily be limited to, one-on-one conferences, parent or faculty advisory committees, student council, suggestion box, and quality circles.

Scale of Descriptors

1. No information is collected from staff, parents, and students. Principal is unresponsive to concerns of these groups.

2. Although information is sporadically collected from groups, principal is largely ineffective in responding to concerns.

3. Information is systematically collected from at least one of the three groups, and the principal is effective in responding to concerns.

4. Information is systematically collected from at least two of the three groups, and the principal is effective in responding to concerns.

5. Information is systematically collected from parents, faculty, and students; the principal is effective in responding to concerns; and the information is used in planning and implementing change.

Key Points in Descriptors

1. No information; unresponsive principal.

2. Sporadic information; ineffective principal.

3. Systematic information from one group; effective principal.

4. Systematic information from two groups; effective principal.

5. Systematic information from three groups; effective principal; use of information to plan change.

Indicator 7.7

Acknowledges appropriately the meaningful accomplishments of others.

Comment

The main focus in Indicator 7.7 is the variety of activities engaged in by the principal that demonstrate the ability to recognize the contributions of staff, students, and parents. Activities might include, but not necessarily be limited to, staff recognition programs, student award assemblies, certificates, congratulatory notes, phone calls, recognition luncheons, and newspaper articles.

Scale of Descriptors

1. Principal engages in no recognition activities.

2. Principal engages in at least one recognition activity for one of the three groups (staff, parents, students).

3. Principal engages in at least one recognition activity for two of the three groups (staff, parents, students).

4. Principal engages in at least one recognition activity for all three groups (staff, parents, students).

5. In addition to a variety of recognition activities, the principal involves all three groups in recognition activities for one another.

Key Points in Descriptors

1. No recognition activities

2. One recognition for one of three groups

3. One recognition for two of three groups

4. One recognition for all three groups

5. Many recognition activities, with focus on groups recognizing each other

Conclusion

WHAT ARE THE SEVEN STEPS?

In the Introduction, I suggested several obstacles to becoming an effective instructional leader—lack of skills and training; lack of time; lack of teacher cooperation; lack of support from superintendents, school boards, and community; and lack of vision, will, or courage. But I also noted that anyone with the desire—*ganas*—could leap over tall buildings in a single bound. Implementing the seven steps to effective instructional leadership is not something you are going to do to your school or teachers but something you are going to do to yourself. Let's briefly review the seven steps and then look at how you might begin their implementation.

Step One: Establish, Implement, and Achieve Academic Standards

This step involves what Stephen Covey calls beginning with the end in mind. Knowing what you want the graduates of your school to be able to know and do, and then making sure that your students acquire that knowledge and those skills, is the heart of the whole schooling enterprise—our *raison d'être. The focus of step one is on knowing where you are going—the destination of your journey—and then being able to determine if you have arrived.* Where will the wagons be heading when they pull out of the last outpost?

> [What we need to do is] turn the reflection of the school principal to the core technology of schooling—teaching and learning—and achieve the same level of reflection on curriculum, program development, and instruction that may well already go on with less important or critical matters.
>
> (Smith & Andrews, 1989, p. 4)

Step Two: Be an Instructional Resource for Your Staff

This step has less to do with offering support to teachers if they are feeling blue or need a shoulder to cry on than with being an instructional resource who provides the kind of encouragement, motivation, and solid

> The first step toward effectiveness is to decide what are the right things to do. Efficiency, which is doing things right, is irrelevant until you work on the right things.
>
> (Drucker, 1990, p. 198)

observational feedback that teachers need to improve their teaching. *The focus of step two is making sure that the people with whom you are traveling know where they can go for help whenever they need it.* When the wagon breaks down or the provisions run short, be there to shoot that wild turkey for dinner or replace a broken wagon wheel.

Step Three: Create a School Culture and Climate Conducive to Learning

> Leaders know what they want, why they want it, and how to communicate what they want to others, in order to gain their cooperation and support.
>
> (Bennis, 1989, p. 3)

Your assignment in step three is to make sure that everything that happens in your school is focused on one goal—learning. Time is being used effectively, programs and activities facilitate learning, and expectations are high. *The focus of step three is making sure that nothing interferes with reaching your destination.* Through buffalo stampedes and raging rapids, press on, refusing to be deterred or distracted by the obstacles and barriers.

Step Four: Communicate the Vision and Mission of Your School

We all lose our way at times. We become distracted by failure, competing agendas, personal problems, or trivial goals. Step four simply means that you will continually find ways to reassert, rephrase, refocus, and revitalize your mission. *The focus of step four is making sure that nobody forgets the goal (the destination of the journey).* Circulate through the camp each night to talk about the glories of unexplored lands, the excitement of walking through uncharted territories, and retell the story of the triumphs over tragedy that have already occurred on the trip.

Step Five: Set High Expectations for Your Staff and Yourself

> Renewal is the principle—and the process—that empowers us to move on an upward spiral of growth and change, on continuous improvement.
>
> (Covey, 1989, p. 304)

Teachers serve at the critical point of instructional delivery. They need to be peak performers every minute of every day. You cannot do their job for them, but you can help them reach those performance pinnacles through observation, feedback, mentoring, and coaching. *The focus of step five is making sure that all the pioneers have the tools and talents to go with you on the journey.* Encourage all members of the caravan to do their very best, offering words of encouragement and assistance whenever needed.

Step Six: Develop Teacher Leaders

Teachers have a dual role to play in reaching the goal of learning for all students. Not only are they responsible for managing instruction but they also have a role to play in both decision making and leadership. *The focus of step six is making sure that everyone shares the leadership and responsibility for reaching the destination.* When you grow weary, ask others to act as wagon master, resting secure in the knowledge that they are well prepared.

Step Seven: Establish and Maintain Positive Relationships With Students, Staff, and Parents

While you, the instructional leader, are doing all the big important things of leadership, (e.g., setting goals, communicating the mission, setting high expectations, and bringing out the leader in everyone), please do remember what's really important—the people. *The focus of step seven is about making sure that all the while you are striving for the goal (destination), the relationships of the folks who are traveling together will not be overlooked.* Through the difficult moments that are stressful, anxious, and irritating, the journey will, nevertheless, be characterized by good times around the campfire and satisfaction at pulling through the mud holes as a team. Have some fun along the way. Strong instructional leadership will make the difference.

> Intimacy rises from translating personal and corporate values into daily work practices, from searching for knowledge and wisdom and justice. Above all, intimacy is one way of describing the relationship we all desire with work.
>
> (DePree, 1989, p. 49)

WHAT CAN YOU DO TO GET STARTED?

Don't put off until tomorrow what really needs to begin today. Think now about what you can do to change your instructional leadership behaviors. Some of the things effective, experienced instructional leaders do are described below.

> You can and should shape your own future, because if you don't someone else surely will.
>
> (Barker, 1992, p. 21)

Self-Assess Your Instructional Leadership Behaviors

Spend a few moments, now that you have completed this book, to use the Instructional Leadership Checklist (Resource A) and Response Form (Resource B) to assess yourself. Be honest in your appraisal, and use the information from your self-reflection to help you set personal and professional goals.

Ask Your Staff to Assess Your Instructional Leadership Behaviors

Thinking is the most important act of leadership in a change-oriented environment.

(Schlechty, 1990, p. 98)

Don't wait for others to tell you where you need to improve. Ask them. When I first began this process, it was painful. I divided my faculty into four groups—one group for each of my building leadership team members. They summarized the answers to each of these questions: "What am I doing that is effective and should be continued? What am I doing that is ineffective and should be stopped? What am I not doing that I should be doing?" I met with all team members individually, and they shared with me what the teachers in their groups had said. There were moments of pain and disbelief. Surely I couldn't be like that? Didn't they know how hard I worked and how much I did?

In addition to requesting informal verbal feedback from your staff, ask them to use all or parts of the Instructional Leadership Checklist to rate your leadership behaviors. Discuss the results with your leadership team, and use them to plan improvement initiatives.

Work and Network With Colleagues

The most exciting thing about preparing this manuscript was reading the questionnaires and talking in person with many of the instructional leaders who contributed. They are an impressive and awe-inspiring group of individuals. People like them work in every community and state. Find one or two strong instructional leaders in your area. Talk to them, shadow them, and pick their brains at every opportunity. Join professional organizations (both state and national), and volunteer for committees.

Attend Classes

If you do not already have one, begin to work on an advanced degree. Barth (cited in Sparks, 1993) chides principals not to become the at-risk principal who, like the at-risk student, "leaves school before or after graduation with little possibility of continuing learning" (p. 19). While every class won't inspire you, the contacts with other educators, the opportunities for thinking and reading, and the challenge of being a learner yourself will. Spend part of every summer in a professional institute experience. Many instructional leaders have attended the Harvard Principals Center or workshops and training opportunities sponsored by the National Association of Elementary School Principals (NAESP) or the National Association of Secondary School Principals (NASSP)—with astounding results in their personal and professional lives.

Read Books

You may already have an advanced degree, but that should not keep you from learning. Become a student of the leadership literature. Acquire the books on the must-read lists throughout this book, and begin to work your way through the stack. Ask a group of principals from your district or your area to join you in a once-a-month book club luncheon.

Subscribe to Journals and Newspapers and Read Them

My favorites are *Education Week*, *Educational Leadership*, *NASSP Bulletin*, *Principal*, and *Phi Delta Kappan*.

Set Goals

If you are not currently setting short-term, long-term, and visionary goals in all areas of your life—career, education, family, social, and spiritual, you are missing out on some real benefits in your life. In its Aspiring Principals Workshop, NAESP suggests that establishing goals will help you to

- Break out of that being-in-a-rut feeling
- Reduce the frequency of down days
- Help stretch peak days
- Tap unused potential
- Stretch thinking
- Reduce procrastination
- Develop a winning attitude
- Rediscover optimism
- Make better use of your subconscious
- Become more self-motivated

Take Risks

I have taken some big risks in my day. I volunteered to bring a teacher and her class to be observed by 125 other administrators and then agreed to conduct a conference with her in front of them. I challenged the CEO at a multinational company in our attendance area to trade places with me for a day. Both of these risks resulted in opportunities for my students and teachers that I could never have foreseen. Although the adage says "think before you act," there are many occasions when we ponder too long over the ramifications of something and fail to seize the moment.

Volunteer to Teach a Class or Workshop

Jim Blockinger has taught Administrators' Academies in the areas of supervision and instructional leadership. Although Jim's academies have helped countless Illinois administrators to improve, no one has improved more from his classes than Jim.

Join Professional Organizations and Become Active

Become affiliated with the NAESP, NASSP, the National Middle School Principals, or the Association for Supervision and Curriculum Development. Join the state affiliates of these organizations as well. Attend meetings. Volunteer for committees. Rubbing shoulders with other instructional leaders in your state and nation will enlarge your horizons and expand your vision.

Think and Reflect on Your Own Practice of the Principalship

If you are moving through your work without constant reflection on all the things that are happening, you are missing out on wonderful learning opportunities.

Effective instructional leaders are never satisfied. They always want more—from themselves, their teachers, and their students. They are learning something new every day. They know they can't expect their teachers to give them more than they themselves are willing to give, and they're constantly aware that everyone is watching to see if they are walking their talk.

Many instructional leaders have had to learn patience. Although they are motivated, are driven to accomplish what they know needs to be done, and have a vision for the future, they recognize the folly of bulldozing a plan. Nancy Carbone explains it in this way: "You have to believe in the process and have patience with people." She elaborates, "I found that if I presented the information for people in a variety of ways and trusted their instincts to do the right thing, they would not disappoint me." Instructional leaders have also learned that their work is never really done. For task-oriented individuals who want to cross things off their proverbial lists, instructional leadership means never being finished. Alan Jones summarized it rather neatly: "You really need patience. Profound change takes 5 to 7 years. Change is not a rational process. You just have to have a vision and then hang on for the ride!"

CHALLENGE FOR THE FUTURE

Begin today to change some of the ways you do business in your school. The research is clear. How you act every day makes a difference in the educational lives of students. Through the words you use, the actions you choose, and the vision you pursue, you *will* make a major impact on student learning. The question is not if you *are* or *will* have an impact on the students, parents, and teachers with whom you work. The question is *what kind* of an impact will you make. Altering even a few instructional leadership behaviors will produce dramatic results in the effectiveness of your teachers, the support of your community, the learning of your students, and the personal satisfaction you'll feel from having made a difference.

> Futurists have a tantalizing way of describing the [future] as though being there has little to do with getting there. The future simply arrives full-blown. But it is the succession of days and years between now and then that will determine what life will be like. Decisions made and not made will shape the schools of tomorrow.
>
> (Goodlad, 1984, p. 321)

Read through scales.

Rate 1-5.

Average the scores for each indicator.

Resource A: Instructional Leadership Checklist

STEP ONE: ESTABLISH, IMPLEMENT, AND ACHIEVE ACADEMIC STANDARDS

There are four indicators that describe step one in more detail. Each indicator is followed by three sections: (a) a *comment* that defines the specific focus of the indicator; (b) a *scale of descriptors* that gives a continuum of behaviors (1 to 5) from least effective to most effective; and (c) *key points in the descriptors* that give succinct explanations of each of the five items in the scale. For each indicator, select the number from 1 to 5 that most accurately describes your own behavior on a day-to-day basis.

Indicator 1.1

Incorporates the designated state and district standards into the development and implementation of the local school's instructional programs.

Comment

The main focus of Indicator 1.1 is the support the principal gives to mandated state and district standards while developing and implementing an instructional program that also meets the needs of the individual students, classrooms, and the school as a whole.

Scale of Descriptors

1. Principal does not support the use of state and district standards as the basis for the instructional program.

2. Principal pays lip service to the use of state and district standards as the basis for the school's instructional program but permits teachers to exercise personal judgments regarding their ultimate inclusion.

3. Principal believes that state and district standards should be used as the basis for the school's instructional program and communicates these expectations to teachers.

4. Principal believes that state and district standards should be the basis for the school's instructional program, communicates these expectations to teachers, and works with them in the development of instructional programs that do this effectively.

5. Principal believes that state and district standards should be the basis for the school's instructional program, communicates these expectations to teachers, works with them in the development of instructional programs that do this effectively, and monitors classroom activities and instruction to ensure such inclusion.

Key Points in Descriptors

1. No incorporation of state or district standards into program

2. Belief in importance but permissive in supervision

3. Belief in importance with expectations communicated

4. Belief in importance, expectations communicated, and assistance provided

5. Belief in importance, expectations communicated, assistance provided, and implementation monitored

Indicator 1.2

Ensures that schoolwide and individual classroom instructional activities are consistent with state, district, and school standards and are articulated and coordinated with one another.

Comment

The main focus of Indicator 1.2 is the match between the highest level of academic standards—whether those be state, school, or district—and what is happening in individual classrooms and the school as a whole; and what the principal is doing to ensure that consistency exists in each classroom in the building. The existence of clear standards is a *given* in this indicator.

Scale of Descriptors

1. Although state, district, and school standards do exist, many activities act as deterrents or impediments to the achievement of those standards.

2. Although state, district, and school standards do exist, instructional practices in the school as a whole (majority of classrooms) do not appear to support the achievement of those standards.

3. Although instructional practices in the school as a whole appear to support the state, district, and school standards, there are many individual classrooms in which instructional activities and outcomes do not support the stated standards.

4. Instructional activities and student achievement in *most* classrooms and the school as a whole support the stated standards.

5. Instructional activities in *all* classrooms and the school as a whole support the state, district, and school academic standards.

Key Points in Descriptors

1. Level 1 implies that the principal is unwilling to address a lack of consistency in *many* classrooms (more than half) or in the school as a whole.

2. Level 2 implies that the principal expresses a verbal willingness to address lack of consistency but fails to follow through with actions to ensure consistency.

3. Level 3 implies that the principal is willing to address a lack of consistency between standards and instruction but is marginally effective in doing so.

4. Level 4 implies that the principal is willing to ensure consistency between standards and instruction and is usually very effective in doing so.

5. Level 5 implies that the principal is highly effective in ensuring that instructional activities and outcomes match standards.

Indicator 1.3

Uses multiple sources of data, both qualitative and quantitative, to evaluate progress and plan for continuous improvement.

Comment

The main focus of Indicator 1.3 is the use of multiple assessments and sources of data by the principal and, in turn, the teachers to evaluate and, if necessary, make subsequent adjustments in instruction or curriculum to ensure that state, district, and school academic standards are being achieved.

Scale of Descriptors

1. No internal schoolwide program of assessment or data collection exists.

2. Although a district or schoolwide standardized testing program exists, the results are merely disseminated to teachers and parents; the principal does not use the information to help teachers evaluate and improve the instructional program.

3. Standardized test information is the sole indicator used by the principal for program evaluation. Review of the information is not systematic or specific, and teachers rarely review the results beyond the initial report.

4. Results of multiple-assessment methods—such as ongoing curriculum-based assessments, criterion-referenced tests, standardized tests, and performance or portfolio assessments—are systematically used and reviewed by the principal along with teachers.

5. Results of multiple-assessment methods are systematically used to evaluate program objectives. A schoolwide database that contains longitudinal assessment data for each student, classroom teacher, and grade level, as well as for the whole school, is regularly used by the principal and teachers to make instructional and program modifications for the school, individual classrooms or grade levels, and individual students, and to set meaningful and measurable goals for subsequent school improvement.

Key Points in Descriptors

1. No testing program

2. Standardized testing program with little use of results by either principal or teachers

3. Standardized testing program with some use of results by principal and little use of results by teachers

4. Well-rounded evaluation program with some use of results by both principal and teachers

5. Well-rounded evaluation program with effective use of results by both principal and teachers to modify and improve program.

Indicator 1.4

Instructional leadership efforts on the part of the principal result in meaningful and measurable achievement gains.

Comment

The main focus of Indicator 1.4 is the achievement of measurable gains on a state assessment or local standardized test as a result of sustained instructional leadership and improvement efforts led by the principal.

Scale of Descriptors

1.   The principal believes instructional leadership is no different from management and is unwilling to devote time and resources to improvement efforts toward raising achievement.

2.   The principal pays lip service to the concept of instructional leadership, the development of goals, and school improvement activities but does nothing to provide resources or support to teachers.

3.   The principal believes that instructional leadership is important, engages in some goal-setting and school improvement activities, but is unable to provide the support and resources that are necessary to bring about change.

4.   The principal believes that instructional leadership is essential, engages in many meaningful goal-setting and school improvement activities, provides some support and resources that have resulted in some measurable achievement gains, but is unable to hold all teachers accountable and sustain improvement or realize meaningful gains for more than 1 year.

5.   The principal believes that instructional leadership is key, engages in meaningful goal-setting and school improvement activities, provides strong support and ample resources, and has led the staff to meaningful achievement gains that have been sustained over time.

Key Points in Descriptors

1. No instructional leadership toward school improvement.

2. Minimal effort given to instructional leadership, goal setting, and school improvement activities. No resources or support provided to teachers. No gains.

3. Some instructional leadership. Some goal-setting and school improvement activities. Limited resources and support. No gains.

4. Excellent instructional leadership. Meaningful goal-setting and school improvement activities. Provision of resources and support. Limited accountability for all teachers. Minimal gains.

5. Strong instructional leadership. Meaningful goal-setting and school improvement activities. Provision of resources and support. Consistent accountability. Sustainable gains.

STEP TWO: BE AN INSTRUCTIONAL RESOURCE FOR YOUR STAFF

There are three indicators that describe this step in more detail. Each indicator is followed by three sections: (a) a *comment* that defines the specific focus of the indicator; (b) a *scale of descriptors* that gives a continuum of behaviors (1 to 5) from least effective to most effective; and (c) *key points in the descriptors* that give succinct explanations of each of the five items in the scale. For each indicator, select the number from 1 to 5 that most accurately describes your own behavior on a day-to-day basis.

Indicator 2.1

Works with teachers to improve instructional programs in their classrooms consistent with student needs.

Comment

The main focus of Indicator 2.1 is the role of the principal as an instructional resource for teachers in solving specific instructional problems related to student learning. Quality and quantity of assistance are to be considered as well as frequency with which teachers call on the principal for assistance.

Scale of Descriptors

1. Principal has no interaction with teachers regarding the instructional program in their classrooms. Principal has almost no understanding of instructional program. Teachers never ask for instructional assistance from the principal, preferring to deal with instructional matters independently.

2. Principal rarely assists teachers with instructional concerns but will attempt to assist a teacher if a specific, well-defined request is

made. Principal has very sketchy knowledge and understanding of the instructional program. Teachers make few requests for assistance.

3. Principal works in a limited way with those few teachers who request help. Principal's knowledge of instructional strategies is basic, and outside resources are often needed to solve instructional problems.

4. Principal works with most teachers through coordination and delegation, showing a strong degree of expertise. Teachers frequently turn to the principal for assistance.

5. Principal works with all teachers on a continuing basis and is an important resource for instructional concerns. The principal frequently initiates interaction, and teachers regularly turn to the principal for help, which is given with a high level of expertise.

Key Points in Descriptors

1. No interaction, no expertise, no requests for assistance
2. Little interaction, limited expertise, few requests for assistance
3. Some interaction, basic expertise, some requests for assistance
4. Frequent interaction, strong expertise, frequent requests for assistance
5. Regular interaction, outstanding expertise, regular requests for assistance.

Indicator 2.2

Facilitates instructional program development based on trustworthy research and proven instructional practices.

Comment

The main focus of Indicator 2.2 is the status of the principal as an active learner in the acquisition of current educational research and practice and how effectively this knowledge base is shared and translated into instructional programs.

Scale of Descriptors

1. Principal is unaware of current, trustworthy educational research and proven practices.

2. Principal may be aware of current, trustworthy educational research and proven practices but feels this body of knowledge has little bearing on the day-to-day functioning of the school.

3. Principal is aware of current, trustworthy educational research and proven practices and believes they should affect program development but is not currently attempting to translate this information into practice.

4. Principal is aware of current, trustworthy educational research and proven practices, believes they should affect program development, shares them actively with staff, and is currently attempting to translate this information into instructional program development.

5. Principal is aware of current, trustworthy educational research and proven practices, believes they should affect program development, shares them actively with staff, and has successfully developed or altered school programs to reflect this knowledge base.

Key Points in Descriptors

1. No awareness of or belief in the importance or use of current educational research

2. Some awareness of but no belief in importance or use of current educational research

3. Some awareness of and belief in importance of but no use of current educational research

4. Awareness of, belief in importance of and some attempts to translate information into instructional program

5. Awareness of, belief in importance of successful implementation of school programs based on research

Indicator 2.3

Uses appropriate formative-assessment procedures and informal data-collection methods for evaluating the effectiveness of instructional programs in achieving state, district, and local standards.

Comment

The main focus of Indicator 2.3 is the combination of multiple methods of evaluation by the principal that are formative in nature and indicate the need for immediate adjustments in instructional strategies, groupings, time allocations, lesson design, and so on. Examples of formative-evaluation tools are teacher-made tests; curriculum-based assessments; samples of student work; mastery-skills checklists; criterion-referenced tests; end-of-unit tests; observations in classrooms; and conversations with teachers, parents, and students.

Scale of Descriptors

1. Principal does not receive any regular, formative-evaluation information from classroom teachers.

2. Principal receives some formative-evaluation information from some classroom teachers, but sharing of this information is voluntary.

3. Principal solicits some formative-evaluation information regularly from all classroom teachers.

4. Principal solicits some formative-evaluation information regularly from all classroom teachers and discusses this information with teachers.

5. Principal solicits comprehensive, formative-evaluation information regularly from all classroom teachers, discusses this information with teachers and, together with teachers, plans for changes in day-to-day classroom practices to increase instructional effectiveness.

Key Points in Descriptors

1. No regular, formative-evaluation information

2. Some voluntary, formative-evaluation information

3. Formative-evaluation information solicited regularly

4. Formative-evaluation information solicited regularly and discussed

5. Formative-evaluation information solicited regularly, discussed, and instructional practices adjusted

STEP THREE: CREATE A SCHOOL CULTURE AND CLIMATE CONDUCIVE TO LEARNING

There are three indicators that describe this step in more detail. Each indicator is followed by three sections: (a) a *comment* that defines the specific focus of the indicator; (b) a *scale of descriptors* that gives a continuum of behaviors (1 to 5) from least effective to most effective; and (c) *key points in the descriptors* that give succinct explanations of each of the five items in the scale. For each indicator, select the number from 1 to 5 that most accurately describes your own behavior on a day-to-day basis.

Indicator 3.1

Establishes high expectations for student achievement that are directly communicated to students, teachers, and parents.

Comment

The main focus of Indicator 3.1 concerns the philosophical assumptions the individual makes about the ability of all students to learn, the need for both equity and excellence in the educational program, and the ability to communicate these beliefs to students, teachers, and parents.

Scale of Descriptors

1. Principal believes that nonalterable variables, such as home background, socioeconomic status, and ability level, are the prime determinants of student achievement, and the school cannot overcome these factors.

2. Principal believes that the nonalterable variables cited above significantly affect student achievement and the school has a limited impact on student achievement.

3. Principal believes that although the nonalterable variables cited above may influence student achievement, teachers are responsible for all students mastering basic skills and prescribed learner outcomes according to individual levels of expectancy. The principal occasionally communicates these expectations in an informal way to teachers, parents, and students via written and spoken communications or specific activities.

4. Principal believes that although the nonalterable variables cited above may influence student achievement, teachers are responsible for all students mastering certain basic skills at their grade level, and frequently communicates these expectations to teachers, parents, and students in a formal, organized manner. Expectations for student achievement may be communicated through written statements of objectives in basic skills or a written statement of purpose and mission for the school that guides the instructional program.

5. Principal believes that together the home and school can have a profound influence on student achievement. Teachers are held responsible not only for all students mastering certain basic skills at their grade level but also for the stimulation, enrichment, and acceleration of the

student who is able to learn more quickly and the provision of extended learning opportunities for students who may need more time for mastery. Expectations for student achievement are developed jointly among parent, student, and teacher and are communicated not only through written statements of learner outcomes in core curriculum areas but also in enriched and accelerated programs, achievement awards, and opportunities for creative expression.

Key Points in Descriptors

1. No impact by school on students. No communication of achievement expectations to teachers, parents, or students.

2. Limited impact by school on students. No communication of achievement expectations to teachers, parents, or students.

3. All students should master basic learner outcomes. Limited communication of achievement expectations to teachers, parents, and students.

4. All students should master basic learner outcomes. Formal communication of achievement expectations to teachers, parents, and students.

5. All students master basic learner outcomes with many students exceeding the minimal competencies, participating in an enriched or accelerated course, and receiving academic awards. Joint development of achievement expectations by teachers, parents, and students.

Indicator 3.2

Establishes clear standards, communicates expectations for the use of time allocated to instruction, and monitors the effective use of classroom time.

Comment

The main focus of Indicator 3.2 is the existence of written guidelines for use of classroom time, the existence of a weekly program schedule for each classroom teacher, the regular monitoring of lesson plans, and the schoolwide schedule and its impact on instructional time.

Scale of Descriptors

1. Teachers are totally unsupervised in the planning of their daily schedule. No written guidelines exist for the use of classroom time. There are frequent interruptions that significantly interfere with instruction.

2. State, district, or school guidelines for the use of classroom time exist, but the principal does not monitor their implementation in the classroom. There are many interruptions to instructional time that could be avoided.

3. State, district, or school guidelines for the use of classroom time exist, and the principal monitors their implementation in the classroom by requiring teachers to post a copy of their weekly schedule and by occasionally reviewing lesson plans. There are some, but not frequent, interruptions.

4. State, district, or school guidelines for the use of classroom time exist; the principal monitors their implementation by requiring teachers to post a weekly program schedule and by regularly reviewing lesson plans. Basic skill instructional time is occasionally interrupted with advance notice. Whenever possible, interruptions are planned during noninstructional time.

5. State, district, or school guidelines for the use of classroom time exist, and the principal monitors regularly their implementation through the review of classroom or grade-level lesson plans and regular classroom visitations. Classroom instructional time is rarely interrupted, and the principal plans with teachers in the coordination of schoolwide schedules to minimize the effect of pullout programs, assemblies, and other special events.

Key Points in Descriptors

1. No guidelines
2. Guidelines, no monitoring, frequent interruptions
3. Guidelines, limited monitoring, limited interruptions
4. Guidelines, frequent monitoring, few interruptions
5. Guidelines, frequent monitoring, coordinated school schedule to minimize interruptions

Indicator 3.3

With teachers and students (as appropriate), establishes, implements, and evaluates procedures and codes for handling and correcting behavior problems.

Comment

The main focus in Indicator 3.3 is the existence of a behavior plan for each classroom and for the building as a whole, and the participation of the principal in the implementation of this plan. The focus of the plan is on responsible, caring behavior by all students and teachers based on mutual respect and common goals. Positive as well as negative reinforcers are included in the plan.

Scale of Descriptors

1. All classroom teachers have their own method of handling behavior problems without support or assistance from the principal, and there is no schoolwide behavior plan or comprehensive set of school rules.

2. All classroom teachers have their own methods of handling behavior, and no schoolwide behavior plan or set of school rules exists. The principal is available for assistance with severe behavior problems and handles them on an individual basis with little uniformity or consistency.

3. Each classroom teacher files a behavior plan with the principal, and rules for behavior in common areas of the building are available. The principal is generally supportive and provides assistance with behavior problems.

4. Each classroom teacher files a behavior plan with the principal. Rules for student behavior in common areas of the building have been developed jointly by the principal, teachers, and students (as appropriate) and made available to all parents and students. The principal is consistent and cooperative in implementing the school behavior plan.

5. In addition to individual classroom behavior plans and rules for student behavior in common areas of the building, a buildingwide behavior plan has been developed in which the principal assumes a joint responsibility with all staff members, students, and parents for discipline and school behavior. A climate of mutual respect exists between students, teachers, and principal based on the fair application of the plan.

Key Points in Descriptors

1. No classroom plans, no school rules, no schoolwide plan, no principal support

2. No classroom plans, no school rules, no schoolwide plan, some principal support

3. Classroom plans, school rules, no schoolwide plan, adequate principal support

4. Classroom plans, school rules developed jointly and furnished to students and parents, no schoolwide plan, excellent principal support

5. Classroom plans, school rules developed jointly and furnished to students and parents, schoolwide plan developed jointly and furnished to students and parents, excellent principal support

STEP FOUR: COMMUNICATE THE VISION AND MISSION OF YOUR SCHOOL

There are three indicators that describe this step in more detail. Each indicator is followed by three sections: (a) a *comment* that defines the specific focus of the indicator; (b) a *scale of descriptors* that gives a continuum of behaviors (1 to 5) from least effective to most effective; and (c) *key points in the descriptors* that give succinct explanations of each of the five items in the scale. For each indicator, select the number from 1 to 5 that most accurately describes your own behavior on a day-to-day basis.

Indicator 4.1

Provides for systematic, two-way communication with staff regarding the achievement standards and the improvement goals of the school.

Comment

The main focus of Indicator 4.1 is the provision of two-way communication channels to ensure an ongoing discussion of the mission of the school.

Scale of Descriptors

1. There is no communication between principal and staff regarding the mission of the school.

2. Communication between principal and staff is largely one way and limited to administrative directives regarding principal expectations.

3. Although principal and staff communicate informally regarding the mission of the school, there are no regular two-way communication channels.

4. Two-way communication channels between principal and staff have been established in the form of faculty meetings; grade-level, departmental, and team meetings; and teacher and principal conferences; but these channels are frequently used for administrative or social purposes and are not regularly devoted to a discussion of instructional goals and priorities.

5. Established two-way communication channels are regularly used by the principal as a means of addressing the standards and improvement goals of the school with the staff.

Key Descriptors

1. No communication

2. One-way communication, no established channels

3. Informal two-way communication, no established channels

4. Established channels, no regular use of these channels

5. Regular use of established channels for two-way communication regarding school mission

Indicator 4.2

Establishes, supports, and implements activities that communicate the value and meaning of learning to students.

Comment

The main focus of Indicator 4.2 is the existence of activities that communicate the value of learning to students. Examples of such activities might be awards or honors assemblies, learning-incentive programs, career awareness programs, honor societies, work-study programs, academic clubs, and mentoring or shadowing programs. This list is meant to be suggestive but certainly not inclusive.

Scale of Descriptors

1. No activities exist that communicate the value and meaning of learning to students.

2. At least one activity exists that communicates the value and meaning of learning to students.

3. More than three activities exist that communicate the value and meaning of learning to students.

4. More than six activities exist that communicate the value and meaning of learning to students.

5. More than 10 activities exist that communicate the value and meaning of learning to students.

Key Points in Descriptors

1. No activities

2. One activity

3. More than three activities

4. More than six activities

5. More than 10 activities

Indicator 4.3

Develops and uses communication channels with parents to set forth school objectives.

Comment

The main focus of Indicator 4.3 is the existence of communication channels that are specifically devoted to setting forth standards and school improvement goals to parents. Examples of communication channels might include, but not necessarily be limited to, grade-level curriculum nights; newsletter column devoted specifically to school objectives; parent conferences; written statement of school mission; written statement of standards for each grade level, particularly in the core curricular areas of reading and mathematics; school activities devoted to skill mastery that require parent participation (e.g., contract for parents reading with or aloud to students); and homework policy.

Scale of Descriptors

1. No communication channels to setting forth school objectives exist.

2. At least three communication channels exist to setting forth school objectives.

3. At least six communication channels exist to setting forth school objectives.

4. At least 10 communication channels exist to setting forth school objectives.

5. In addition to the 10 communication channels that exist to setting forth school objectives, the principal and faculty are evaluating, refining, and developing additional means of communicating with parents regarding school objectives.

Key Points in Descriptors

1. No channels

2. At least three channels

3. At least six channels

4. At least 10 channels

5. At least 10 channels and an evaluation, refining, and development process

STEP FIVE: SET HIGH EXPECTATIONS FOR YOUR STAFF AND YOURSELF

There are seven indicators that describe this step in more detail. Each indicator is followed by three sections: (a) a *comment* that defines the specific focus of the indicator; (b) a *scale of descriptors* that gives a continuum of behaviors (1 to 5) from least effective to most effective; and (c) *key points in the descriptors* that give succinct explanations of each of the five items in the scale. For each indicator, select the number from 1 to 5 that most accurately describes your own behavior on a day-to-day basis. (District requirements for frequency and procedures with regard to teacher evaluation may vary and substantially impact the interpretation of step five. In large schools, several administrators may share supervision and evaluation responsibilities. The indicators and their scales of descriptors describes a best-case scenario.)

Indicator 5.1

Assists teachers yearly in setting and reaching personal and professional goals related to the improvement of instruction, student achievement, and professional development.

Comment

The main focus of Indicator 5.1 is the active participation of the principal with teachers in goal-setting and goal-achieving processes. The principal provides assistance to the teachers in reaching stated goals, and the information obtained in the goal-setting process is used in teacher evaluation.

Scale of Descriptors

1. Principal does not require that teachers set personal and professional goals.

2. Principal requires that all teachers develop, in cooperation with the principal, personal and professional goals but is not involved in the goal-setting process and does not require that goals be related to the improvement of instruction and overall school improvement goals.

3. Principal requires that teachers set personal and professional goals and that these goals be related to the improvement of instruction and overall school improvement goals but does not assist in the attainment of goals or monitor completion.

4. Principal requires that all teachers develop, in cooperation with the principal, personal and professional goals, and that these goals be related to the improvement of instruction and overall school improvement goals; provides assistance in the attainment of these goals.

5. Principal requires that all teachers develop, in cooperation with the principal, personal and professional goals related to the improvement of instruction and overall school improvement goals. Principal provides assistance to the teachers in the attainment of goals, monitors the completion of the goals, and uses the information in the evaluation process.

Key Points in Descriptors

1. No goal setting by teachers.

2. Goal setting not necessarily related to the improvement of instruction. No principal input, assistance, monitoring, or evaluation.

3. Goal setting related to improvement of instruction. Principal input. No principal assistance, monitoring, or evaluation.

4. Goal setting related to improvement of instruction. Principal input and assistance. No principal monitoring or evaluation.

5. Goal setting related to improvement of instruction. Principal input, assistance, monitoring, and evaluation.

Indicator 5.2

Makes regular classroom observations in all classrooms, both informal (drop-in visits of varying length with no written or verbal feedback to teacher) and formal (visits where observation data are recorded and communicated to teacher).

Comment

The main focus of Indicator 5.2 is on the quantity of classroom observations (both formal and informal).

Scale of Descriptors

1. Principal makes formal classroom observations once every 3 years or less and never visits the classroom informally.

2. Principal makes at least one formal classroom observation per year and occasionally drops in informally.

3. Principal makes two formal classroom observations per year and at least two monthly informal observations.

4. Principal makes three formal classroom observations per year and at least two monthly informal observations.

5. Principal makes four or more classroom observations per year and visits the classroom informally at least once each week.

Key Points in Descriptors

1. Minimal formal observations and no informal observations

2. One yearly formal observation and minimal informal observations

3. Two yearly formal observations and two monthly informal observations

4. Three yearly formal observations and two monthly informal observations

5. Four yearly formal observations and weekly informal observations.

Indicator 5.3

Engages in planning of classroom observations.

Comment

The main focus of Indicator 5.3 is the quality of pre-observation planning for a formal classroom observation where information is collected relative to improvement of instruction.

Scale of Descriptors

1. There is no typical pattern. Teachers are not usually aware that the principal will visit.

2. The principal generally informs teachers before an observation. A lesson may be observed, but there is no specific request for such on the part of the principal.

3. The principal and teacher arrange together for a specific observation time. A complete lesson is usually observed.

4. The principal and teacher arrange together for a specific observation time. A discussion is held regarding the lesson plan for the observation, but no attempts are ever made by the principal to focus on specific curricular areas or instructional strategies (e.g., cooperative grouping in a reading lesson, questioning techniques used on target students). A complete lesson is always observed.

5. The principal and teacher plan the focus of each observation at a conference. Principal frequently takes the initiative regarding the focus of the observation and relates it to building goals and objectives. A specific observation time is scheduled. A complete lesson is always observed.

Key Points in Descriptors

1. No teacher awareness of observation. No pre-observation planning. Random observation of incomplete lessons.

2. Teacher awareness of observation. No pre-observation planning. Observation includes both complete and incomplete lessons.

3. Teacher awareness of observation. No pre-observation planning. Observation always includes complete lesson.

4. Teacher awareness of observation. Pre-observation planning without specific focus by principal. Complete lesson always observed.

5. Teacher awareness of observation. Pre-observation planning with frequent principal initiative regarding subject of observation. Complete lesson always observed.

Indicator 5.4

Engages in postobservation conferences that focus on the improvement of instruction. (District requirements for frequency and procedures with regard to teacher evaluation may vary and substantially impact the interpretation of this indicator. The scale of descriptors describes a best-case scenario.)

Comment

The main focus of Indicator 5.4 is the quantity and quality of postobservation conferences that focus on the improvement of instruction.

Scale of Descriptors

1. The principal engages in a postobservation conference once every 2 years or less with each teacher, with little to no focus on the improvement of instruction.

2. The principal engages in one postobservation conference with each teacher every year but rarely focuses on the improvement of instruction.

3. The principal engages in two postobservation conferences with each teacher every year and provides one-way information about the improvement of instruction.

4. The principal engages in three postobservation conferences with each teacher every year, engaging in both one-way and two-way communication about the improvement of instruction.

5. The principal engages in four postobservation conferences with each teacher every year, engaging in both one-way and two-way communication about the improvement of instruction. Joint plans for follow-up in the classroom are developed with principal providing instructional resources and assistance.

Key Points in Descriptors

1. One conference every 2 years with little to no focus on improvement of instruction

2. One conference every year with rare focus on improvement of instruction

3. Two conferences every year with one-way communication about improvement of instruction

4. Three conferences every year with both one-way and two-way communication about the improvement of instruction

5. Four conferences every year with both one-way and two-way communication about the improvement of instruction, and joint plans for follow-up with instructional resources and assistance provided

Indicator 5.5

Provides thorough, defensible, and insightful evaluations, making recommendations for personal- and professional-growth goals according to individual needs.

Comment

The main focus of Indicator 5.5 is the quality of the evaluation provided by the principal.

Scale of Descriptors

1. All teachers receive nearly identical written evaluation ratings from the principal. There is no indication that the evaluation is based on direct observation or supporting evidence, and no suggestions for improvement or growth are made.

2. Most teachers receive nearly identical written evaluation ratings from the principal. There is little indication that evaluation is based on direct observation or supporting evidence, and no suggestions for improvement or growth are made.

3. Although gradations of written evaluation ratings exist, these gradations appear to have no relationship to teacher performance or supporting evidence. No suggestions for improvement or growth are made.

4. Most teachers receive thorough written evaluations based on direct observation and supporting evidence. Principal makes few suggestions for improvement and growth.

5. Each teacher receives a thoughtful written evaluation based on direct observation and supporting evidence. Principal includes suggestions for improvement and growth tailored to individual needs.

Key Points in Descriptors

1. Identical evaluations for all teachers. No supporting evidence. No suggestions for growth.

2. Nearly identical evaluations for all teachers. No supporting evidence. No suggestions for growth.

3. Gradation of evaluation ratings. No supporting evidence. No suggestions for growth.

4. Thorough evaluations for all teachers. Supporting evidence. Few suggestions for growth.

5. Thorough evaluations for all teachers. Supporting evidence. Suggestions for growth.

Indicator 5.6

Engages in direct teaching in the classrooms.

Comment

The main focus of Indicator 5.6 is the number of times the principal teaches a lesson observed by a classroom teacher. This indicator does not include reading stories aloud or assisting teachers. It focuses on lesson preparation and the opportunity for the classroom teacher to engage in an observation of the principal teaching this lesson.

Scale of Descriptors

1. Principal engages in no direct teaching in the classroom.

2. Principal engages in direct teaching in any classroom at least once per year.

3. Principal engages in direct teaching in any classroom at least two to four times per year.

4. Principal engages in direct teaching in any classroom at least five to ten times per year.

5. Principal engages in direct teaching in the classroom more than 10 times per year.

Key Points in Descriptors

1. No direct teaching

2. One episode of direct teaching

3. Two to four episodes of direct teaching

4. Five to ten episodes of direct teaching

5. More than 10 episodes of direct teaching

Indicator 5.7

Principal holds high expectations for personal instructional leadership behavior, regularly solicits feedback (both formal and informal) from staff members regarding instructional leadership abilities, and uses such feedback to set yearly performance goals.

Comment

The main focus of Indicator 5.7 is the regularity with which principals solicit input from staff members regarding their own performance and the attention paid to this input with regard to goal setting and genuine attempts to change unproductive behaviors.

Scale of Descriptors

1. Principal does not consider instructional leadership a reliable construct on which to be evaluated by staff members and solicits no input from them relative to own performance.

2. Principal considers instructional leadership to be a reliable evaluative construct and occasionally solicits feedback from staff members relative to own performance but does not use this feedback to set goals.

3. Principal considers instructional leadership to be a reliable evaluative construct, solicits feedback (both formal and informal) from staff members relative to own performance, and makes sporadic attempts to use this information to set goals to change own leadership behavior.

4. Principal considers instructional leadership to be a reliable evaluative construct, solicits feedback (both formal and informal) from staff members relative to own performance, sets yearly performance goals, and can be observed by faculty regularly adding productive leadership behaviors, but is resistant to changing unproductive behaviors.

5. Principal considers instructional leadership to be a reliable evaluative construct, solicits feedback (both formal and informal) from staff members relative to own performance, sets yearly performance goals, can be observed by faculty regularly adding productive leadership behaviors and eliminating unproductive behaviors.

Key Points

1. No feedback solicited from staff members.

2. Some feedback solicited from staff members. No goal setting.

3. Feedback regularly solicited from staff members. Inconsistent use of feedback data to set goals.

4. Regular feedback. Regular goal setting. Addition of productive leadership behaviors. Resistance to elimination of unproductive behaviors.

5. Regular feedback. Regular goal setting. Addition of productive leadership behaviors. Elimination of unproductive behaviors.

STEP SIX: DEVELOP TEACHER LEADERS

There are three indicators that describe this step in more detail. Each indicator is followed by three sections: (a) a *comment* that defines the specific focus of the indicator; (b) a *scale of descriptors* that gives a continuum of behaviors (1 to 5) from least effective to most effective; and (c) *key points in the descriptors* that give succinct explanations of each of the five items in the scale. For each indicator, select the number from 1 to 5 that most accurately describes your own behavior on a day-to-day basis.

Indicator 6.1

Schedules, plans, or facilitates regular meetings of all types (planning, problem solving, decision making, or inservice and training) with and among teachers to address instructional issues.

Comment

The main focus of Indicator 6.1 is both the quantity and quality of meetings that discuss instructional issues.

Scale of Descriptors

1. Few meetings are held, instructional issues are never discussed, and no shared decision making or collaboration is evident.

2. Meetings are held on an as-needed basis, instructional issues are rarely discussed, and no shared decision making or collaboration is evident.

3. Meetings are regularly scheduled, instructional issues are sometimes discussed, and some shared decision making or collaboration is evident.

4. Meetings are regularly scheduled, instructional issues are discussed on an as-needed basis, and some shared decision making and collaboration are evident.

5. Meetings of all types are regularly scheduled, and instructional issues are discussed on a continuing basis. Shared decision making and collaboration characterize all meetings.

Key Points in Descriptors

1. Few meetings held. No instructional discussions. No shared decision making or collaboration.

2. Few meetings held. Rare instructional discussions. No shared decision making collaboration.

3. Regularly scheduled meetings. Some instructional discussions. Some shared decision making and collaboration.

4. Regularly scheduled meetings. Regularly scheduled instructional discussions. Some shared decision making and collaboration.

5. Regularly scheduled meetings with continuing discussion of instructional issues.

Indicator 6.2

Provides opportunities for, and training in, collaboration, shared decision making, coaching, mentoring, curriculum development, and presentations.

Comment

The main focus of Indicator 6.2 is the provision of opportunities, as well as provision of training, in all areas of teacher leadership.

Scale of Descriptors

1. Principal never provides opportunities or training for teachers to develop leadership skills.

2. Principal provides some opportunities and training for teachers to develop leadership skills but does so in a highly controlled and regulated fashion.

3. Principal provides some opportunities and training for teachers to develop leadership skills but permits a great deal of latitude in the exercise of these skills and does not use them or focus them in an organized way.

4. Principal provides multiple opportunities and training for teachers to develop leadership skills and uses these skills to improve instruction, coordinate with building the mission, and improve student learning.

5. Principal provides multiple opportunities and training for teachers to develop leadership skills, uses them to continually improve instruction in classrooms, and has a school leadership team that participates in the continual improvement of the school.

Key Points in Descriptors

1. No opportunities or training.

2. Some opportunities and training but not relevant to needs.

3. Opportunities and training provided that are relevant to faculty needs.

4. Opportunities and training provided that are relevant to faculty needs and relate to improvement of instruction.

5. Opportunities and training provided that are relevant to faculty needs; relate to improvement of instruction; are jointly planned, evaluated, and followed up; and include a systematic school improvement process under the leadership of a school team.

Indicator 6.3

Provides motivation and resources for faculty members to engage in professional-growth activities.

Comment

The focus of Indicator 6.3 is the encouragement provided by the principal to faculty members either by personal example or positive reinforcement as well as the allocation of available resources to support professional-growth activities.

Scale of Descriptors

1. Principal never engages in personal professional-growth activities and discourages teachers from doing so by failing to allocate resources for this activity in the budget.

2. Principal never engages in personal professional-growth activities and although monies are available for teacher activities, does not motivate or positively reinforce those teachers who do so.

3. Principal engages in personal professional-growth activities and allocates resources for teachers to do so as well, but does not motivate or positively reinforce those teachers who do so.

4. Principal engages in personal professional-growth activities, allocates resources for teachers to do so as well, and motivates and positively reinforces those teachers who do so.

5. Principal engages in personal professional-growth activities, allocates available resources for teachers to do so as well, motivates teachers to engage in activities that will benefit the building's instructional program, and uses expertise in sharing with other teachers.

Key Points in Descriptors

1. No personal professional-growth activities; no motivation or reinforcement; no resources for teachers.

2. No personal professional-growth activities; no motivation or reinforcement; some allocation of resources.

3. Personal professional-growth activities; allocation of resources; no motivation or reinforcement.

4. Personal professional-growth activities; allocation of available resources, motivation, and reinforcement.

5. Personal professional-growth activities; allocation of resources, motivation, and reinforcement; use of teachers in building activities.

STEP SEVEN: ESTABLISH AND MAINTAIN POSITIVE RELATIONSHIPS WITH STUDENTS, STAFF, AND PARENTS

There are seven indicators that describe this step in more detail. Each indicator is followed by three sections: (a) a *comment* that defines the specific focus of the indicator; (b) a *scale of descriptors* that gives a continuum of behaviors (1 to 5) from least effective to most effective; and (c) *key points in the descriptors* that give succinct explanations of each of the five items in the scale. For each indicator, select the number from 1 to 5 that most accurately describes your own behavior on a day-to-day basis.

Indicator 7.1

Serves as an advocate for students and communicates with them regarding their school life.

Comment

The main focus of Indicator 7.1 is the behaviors that the principal exhibits that give evidence of student advocacy and interaction with students. Behaviors might include lunch with individual students or groups; frequent appearances on the playground, in the lunchroom, and in the hallways; sponsorship of clubs; availability to students who wish to discuss instructional or disciplinary concerns; knowledge of students' names and family relationships; addressing the majority of students by name; and willingness to listen to the students' side in a faculty-student problem. The preceding list is *only* meant to be suggestive of the types of behaviors that might be appropriate for consideration in this category.

Scale of Descriptors

1. Principal does not feel that acting as a student advocate is an appropriate role of the principal and never interacts with students.

2. Principal does not feel that acting as a student advocate is an appropriate role of the principal and seldom interacts with students.

3. Principal does not feel that acting as a student advocate is an appropriate role of the principal but regularly engages in at least three behaviors that encourage communication between student and principal.

4. Principal feels that acting as a student advocate is an appropriate role of the principal and regularly engages in at least six behaviors that encourage communication between student and principal.

5. Principal feels that acting as a student advocate is an appropriate role of the principal, regularly engages in at least six behaviors that encourage communication between student and principal, and has established some means of receiving input from students regarding their opinions of school life.

Key Points in Descriptors

1. No role as an advocate; no interaction with students.

2. No role as an advocate; rare interaction with students.

3. No role as an advocate; three behaviors that encourage communication.

4. Role as student advocate; six behaviors that encourage communication.

5. Role as an advocate; six behaviors that encourage communication; some means of receiving student input.

Indicator 7.2

Encourages open communication among staff members and maintains respect for differences of opinion.

Comment

The main focus of Indicator 7.2 is the behaviors the principal exhibits that give evidence of maintenance of open communication among staff members and respect for differences of opinion. Behaviors might include open-door policy in the principal's office, acceptance of unpopular ideas and negative feedback from faculty, provision of channels for faculty members to voice grievances or discuss problems, or provision of channels for faculty members to discuss their work with each other. The preceding list is *only* meant to be suggestive of the types of behaviors that might be appropriate for consideration in this category.

Scale of Descriptors

1. Principal does not encourage open communication among staff members and considers differences of opinion to be a sign of disharmony among organizational members.

2. Principal supports open communication but is seldom available for informal encounters with staff members. Appointments must be scheduled, meeting agendas are tightly maintained, and the flow of information and opinions is artificially controlled.

3. Principal supports open communication and is available for informal encounters with staff members. Principal is not responsive, however, to problems, questions, or disagreements and shuts off communication of this nature.

4. Principal supports open communication and is available for informal encounters with staff members. Principal is responsive to problems, questions, or disagreements and encourages staff members to work through differences of opinion in positive ways.

5. Principal supports open communication and is available for informal encounters with staff members. An open-door policy exists with regard to all problems, questions, and disagreements. Principal structures a variety of opportunities for faculty members to interact both formally and informally, encouraging interaction between grade levels, departments, and instructional teams.

Key Points in Descriptors

1. Discourages open communication.

2. Exhibits few behaviors that encourage open communication.

3. Exhibits some behaviors that encourage open communication.

4. Exhibits many behaviors that encourage open communication and facilitates problem solving among staff members.

5. Exhibits many behaviors that encourage open communication; facilitates problem solving among staff members; and structures many opportunities for staff interaction.

Indicator 7.3

Demonstrates concern and openness in the consideration of teacher, parent, and student problems and participates in the resolution of such problems where appropriate.

Comment

The main focus of Indicator 7.3 is the behaviors the principal exhibits in the consideration and resolution of problems.

Scale of Descriptors

1. Principal does not wish to be involved in the consideration of teacher, parent, and student problems.

2. Principal is willing to be involved in the consideration of teacher, parent, and student problems but is largely ineffective because of poor communication and human relations skills.

3. Principal is willing to be involved in the consideration of teacher, parent, and student problems and is sometimes effective in bringing problems to resolution. Exhibits average communication and human relations skills.

4. Principal is willing to be involved in the consideration of teacher, parent, and student problems and is usually effective in bringing problems to resolution. Exhibits excellent communication and human relations skills.

5. Principal is willing to be involved in the consideration of teacher, parent, and student problems and is nearly always effective in bringing problems to resolution. Exhibits outstanding communication and human relations skills. Has established procedures jointly with faculty for the resolution of problems.

Key Points in Descriptors

1. No involvement.

2. Some involvement; ineffective problem solver.

3. Involvement; average problem-solving skills.

4. Involvement; excellent problem-solving skills.

5. Involvement; outstanding problem-solving skills.

Indicator 7.4

Models appropriate human relations skills.

Comment

The main focus of Indicator 7.4 is the variety of appropriate human relations skills that are exhibited by the principal. Behaviors *must* include, but not necessarily be limited to, establishing a climate of trust and security for students and staff; respecting the rights of students, parents, and staff; handling individual relationships tactfully and with understanding; and accepting the dignity and worth of individuals without regard to appearance, race, creed, sex, disability, ability, or social status.

Scale of Descriptors

1. Principal has almost no human relations skills.

2. Principal has marginal human relations skills.

3. Principal has average human relations skills.

4. Principal has excellent human relations skills.

5. Principal has outstanding human relations skills.

Key Points in Descriptors

1. Principal exhibits none of the behaviors listed for this indicator under Comment.

2. Principal exhibits only one or two behaviors listed for this indicator under Comment and often has difficulty with tasks that involve human interaction.

3. Principal exhibits two or three of the behaviors listed for this indicator under Comment and is usually successful with tasks that involve human interaction.

4. Principal exhibits three or four of the behaviors listed for this indicator under Comment and is frequently successful with tasks that involve human interaction.

5. Principal exhibits all of the behaviors listed for this indicator under Comment as well as many other behaviors associated with good human relations and is almost always successful with tasks that involve human interaction.

Indicator 7.5

Develops and maintains high morale.

Comment

The main focus of Indicator 7.5 is the variety of behaviors exhibited by the principal that contribute to the development and maintenance of high morale. Behaviors might include, but not necessarily be limited to, involvement of staff in planning, encouragement of planned social events, openness in the dissemination of information, equity in the division of responsibility and allocation of resources, opportunities for achievement, recognition for achievements, involvement of the staff in problem solving, and assistance and support with personal and professional problems.

Scale of Descriptors

1. Morale is nonexistent in the school building. Principal exhibits none of the behaviors listed in the Comment section for this indicator. There is little unity among staff members, leading to competition, clique formation, destructive criticism, disagreement, and quarreling.

2. Morale is marginal in the school building. Principal exhibits few of the behaviors listed in the Comment section for this indicator. Although fewer visible signs of disunity are evident, faculty members, nevertheless, do not work well together or have positive feelings about their work.

3. Morale is average. Although there are no visible signs of disunity (such as those listed in Descriptor 1 of this scale), teachers work largely as individuals, seldom working together cooperatively with enthusiasm and positive feelings.

4. Morale is excellent. Morale-building behaviors by the principal result in teachers working together to share ideas and resources, to identify instructional problems, to define mutual goals, and to coordinate their activities.

5. Morale is outstanding. Morale-building behaviors by the principal result in teachers working together in a highly effective way while gaining personal satisfaction from their work. Principal has identified specific activities that build morale and systematically engages in these activities.

Key Points in Descriptors

1. Nonexistent morale

2. Marginal morale

3. Average morale

4. Excellent morale

5. Outstanding morale

Indicator 7.6

Systematically collects and responds to staff, parent, and student concerns.

Comment

The main focus of Indicator 7.6 is the responsiveness of the principal to the concerns of staff, parents, and students that have been systematically collected. Examples of vehicles used to collect information might include, but not necessarily be limited to, one-on-one conferences, parent or faculty advisory committees, student council, suggestion box, and quality circles.

Scale of Descriptors

1. No information is collected from staff, parents, and students. Principal is unresponsive to concerns of these groups.

2. Although information is sporadically collected from groups, principal is largely ineffective in responding to concerns.

3. Information is systematically collected from at least one of the three groups, and the principal is effective in responding to concerns.

4. Information is systematically collected from at least two of the three groups, and the principal is effective in responding to concerns.

5. Information is systematically collected from parents, faculty, and students; the principal is effective in responding to concerns; and the information is used in planning and implementing change.

Key Points in Descriptors

1. No information; unresponsive principal.

2. Sporadic information; ineffective principal.

3. Systematic information from one group; effective principal.

4. Systematic information from two groups; effective principal.

5. Systematic information from three groups; effective principal; use of information to plan change.

Indicator 7.7

Acknowledges appropriately the meaningful accomplishments of others.

Comment

The main focus in Indicator 7.7 is the variety of activities engaged in by the principal that demonstrate the ability to recognize the contributions of staff, students, and parents. Activities might include, but not necessarily be limited to, staff recognition programs, student award assemblies, certificates, congratulatory notes, phone calls, recognition luncheons, and newspaper articles.

Scale of Descriptors

1. Principal engages in no recognition activities.

2. Principal engages in at least one recognition activity for one of the three groups (staff, parents, students).

3. Principal engages in at least one recognition activity for two of the three groups (staff, parents, students).

4. Principal engages in at least one recognition activity for all three groups (staff, parents, students).

5. In addition to a variety of recognition activities, the principal involves all three groups in recognition activities for one another.

Key Points in Descriptors

1. No recognition activities

2. One recognition for one of three groups

3. One recognition for two of three groups

4. One recognition for all three groups

5. Many recognition activities, with focus on groups recognizing each other

Resource B: Instructional Leadership Checklist Response Form

INSTRUCTIONAL LEADERSHIP CHECKLIST RESPONSE FORM				
NEVER	SELDOM	SOMETIMES	USUALLY	ALWAYS

Step One: Establishes, implements, and achieves academic standards.

Indicator 1.1　　1　　　2　　　3　　　4　　　5
Incorporates the designated state and district standards into the development and implementation of the local school's instructional programs.

Indicator 1.2　　1　　　2　　　3　　　4　　　5
Ensures that schoolwide and individual classroom instructional activities are consistent with state, district, and school standards and are articulated and coordinated with one another.

Indicator 1.3　　1　　　2　　　3　　　4　　　5
Uses multiple sources of data, both qualitative and quantitative, to evaluate progress and plan for continuous improvement.

(Continued)				
NEVER	SELDOM	SOMETIMES	USUALLY	ALWAYS

Indicator 1.4
Instructional leadership efforts on the part of the principal result in meaningful and measurable achievement gains.

Step Two: Is an instructional resource for staff.

Indicator 2.1   1   2   3   4   5
Works with teachers to improve the instructional programs in their classrooms consistent with student needs.

Indicator 2.2   1   2   3   4   5
Facilitates instructional program development based on trustworthy research and proven instructional practices.

Indicator 2.3   1   2   3   4   5
Uses appropriate formative-assessment procedures and informal data-collection methods for evaluating the effectiveness of instructional programs in achieving state, district, and local standards.

Step Three: Creates a school culture and climate conducive to learning.

Indicator 3.1   1   2   3   4   5
Establishes high expectations for student achievement that are directly communicated to students, teachers, and parents.

Indicator 3.2   1   2   3   4   5
Establishes clear standards, communicates expectations for the use of time allocated to instruction, and monitors the effective use of classroom time.

Indicator 3.3   1   2   3   4   5
With teachers and students (as appropriate), establishes, implements, and evaluates the procedures and codes for handling and correcting behavior problems.

Step Four: Communicates the vision and mission of the school.

Indicator 4.1   1   2   3   4   5
Provides for systematic, two-way communication with staff regarding the achievement standards and the improvement goals of the school.

	NEVER	SELDOM	SOMETIMES	USUALLY	ALWAYS
(Continued)					

	NEVER	SELDOM	SOMETIMES	USUALLY	ALWAYS
Indicator 4.2	1	2	3	4	5

Establishes, supports, and implements activities that communicate the value and meaning of learning to students.

	NEVER	SELDOM	SOMETIMES	USUALLY	ALWAYS
Indicator 4.3	1	2	3	4	5

Develops and uses communication channels with parents to set forth school objectives.

Step Five: Sets high expectations for staff and yourself.

	NEVER	SELDOM	SOMETIMES	USUALLY	ALWAYS
Indicator 5.1	1	2	3	4	5

Assists teachers yearly in setting and reaching personal and professional goals related to the improvement of instruction, student achievement, and professional development.

	NEVER	SELDOM	SOMETIMES	USUALLY	ALWAYS
Indicator 5.2	1	2	3	4	5

Makes regular classroom observations in all classrooms, both informal (drop-in visits of varying length with no written or verbal feedback to teacher) and formal (visits where observation data are recorded and communicated to teacher).

	NEVER	SELDOM	SOMETIMES	USUALLY	ALWAYS
Indicator 5.3	1	2	3	4	5

Engages in planning of classroom observations.

	NEVER	SELDOM	SOMETIMES	USUALLY	ALWAYS
Indicator 5.4	1	2	3	4	5

Engages in postobservation conferences that focus on the improvement of instruction. (District requirements for frequency and procedures with regard to teacher evaluation may vary and substantially impact the interpretation of this indicator. The scale of descriptors describes a best-case scenario.)

	NEVER	SELDOM	SOMETIMES	USUALLY	ALWAYS
Indicator 5.5	1	2	3	4	5

Provides thorough, defensible, and insightful evaluations, making recommendations for personal- and professional-growth goals according to individual needs.

	NEVER	SELDOM	SOMETIMES	USUALLY	ALWAYS
Indicator 5.6	1	2	3	4	5

Engages in direct teaching in the classrooms.

	NEVER	SELDOM	SOMETIMES	USUALLY	ALWAYS
Indicator 5.7	1	2	3	4	5

Principal holds high expectations for personal instructional leadership behavior, regularly solicits feedback (both formal and informal) from staff members regarding instructional leadership abilities, and uses such feedback to set yearly performance goals.

	(Continued)			
NEVER	SELDOM	SOMETIMES	USUALLY	ALWAYS

Step Six: Develops teacher leaders.

Indicator 6.1 1 2 3 4 5
Schedules, plans, or facilitates regular meetings of all types (planning, problem solving, decision making, or inservice and training) with and among teachers to address instructional issues.

Indicator 6.2 1 2 3 4 5
Provides opportunities for, and training in, collaboration, shared decision making, coaching, mentoring, curriculum development, and presentations.

Indicator 6.3 1 2 3 4 5
Provides motivation and resources for faculty members to engage in professional-growth activities.

Step Seven: Establishes and maintains positive relationships with students, staff, and parents.

Indicator 7.1 1 2 3 4 5
Serves as an advocate for students and communicates with them regarding their school life.

Indicator 7.2 1 2 3 4 5
Encourages open communication among staff members and maintains respect for differences of opinion.

Indicator 7.3 1 2 3 4 5
Demonstrates concern and openness in the consideration of teacher, parent, and student problems and participates in the resolution of such problems where appropriate.

Indicator 7.4 1 2 3 4 5
Models appropriate human relations skills.

Indicator 7.5 1 2 3 4 5
Develops and maintains high morale.

Indicator 7.6 1 2 3 4 5
Systematically collects and responds to staff, parent, and student concerns.

Indicator 7.7 1 2 3 4 5
Acknowledges appropriately the meaningful accomplishments of others.

Resource C: ElizaBeth McCay's Assignment

Following is an assignment developed by ElizaBeth McCay, Assistant Professor of Educational Leadership at Virginia Commonwealth University (Richmond, Virginia), for use with *Seven Steps to Effective Instructional Leadership* as a text in Administration 601—Processes of Instructional Leadership.

FROM THE SYLLABUS FOR ADMINISTRATION 601: PROCESSES OF INSTRUCTIONAL LEADERSHIP

Instructional Leadership Assessment and Plan of Improvement

Assessment

Complete the assessment provided in *Seven Steps to Effective Instructional Leadership* to assess the current instructional leadership practices in your school. Utilizing scale of descriptors provided for each area, assess strengths and weaknesses of current practices demonstrated by the principal (or administrative team under the principal's leadership).

Plan of Improvement and Development

Using suggestions provided in the text and from other resources, complete a plan of improvement, specifically highlighting areas receiving a rating of three or fewer. Include in write-up:

• One-paragraph overview of school and principal (including description of instructional leadership team staffing and responsibilities, level and size of school).

- Step number and name; indicator numbers and names.

- Assessment: Assess the overall scoring for the step, using McEwan's Instructional Leadership Checklist (Resource A) (.5 may be added as needed). If scoring varies within a step, explain. Provide an assessment description specific to your situation, in your own words; include concrete examples to illustrate assessment. (Do not restate assessment descriptors from text.)

- Plan for Improvement and Development: list specific suggested activities for improvement and development for each step.

- Summary paragraph regarding overall impressions of instructional leadership in school, based on this assessment, including strengths and weaknesses overall. Include an analysis of overall scores.

- Note: single-spacing is acceptable and suggested for this assignment (approximately 10 to 15 pages).

INSTRUCTIONAL LEADERSHIP ASSESSMENT AND PLAN OF IMPROVEMENT, SAMPLE FORMAT

Note: from the text, copy the steps and indicators. All other writing must be your own (e.g., use scale of descriptors as a guide for your assessment but do not copy into your paper).

Step One: Establish, Implement, and Achieve Academic Standards

Indicator 1.1

Involves teachers in incorporating the designated state or district standards into the development and implementation of the school's instructional programs.

Indicator 1.2:

Indicator 1.3:

Indicator 1.4:

Assessment

Level 3. Only some involvement of teachers. Faculty input is asked for once annually in August faculty meeting and sometimes during school year but without regularity. Principal makes decisions for adoption of curricular materials, sometimes (but not always) based on faculty discussion.

State Outcomes of Learning (SOL) and division curriculum implemented. Examples: include school activities, such as assemblies, that are integrated with goal of improving test-taking skills. Progress toward school and division goals is monitored through. . . .

Plan for Improvement and Development

• Establish curriculum leadership committee within faculty. Create plan for regular meeting (e.g., monthly) to review current curricula, effectiveness, alignment of assessment, district-level initiatives, research on best practices, and training and development needs.

• Establish routines for faculty input to curriculum committee. Create plan for two-way feedback and communication via monthly faculty meetings, committee reports, grade-level meetings with committee representative, and so on.

• Establish comprehensive, long-term staff development plan to address curriculum development needs. For example, if school is reviewing use of technology in subject areas, consider development and implementation of needs assessment, and individually responsive staff development opportunities with in-school consultation in skills and concepts.

• Design peer support system for implementation of curricular objectives. For example, establish peer partnerships between curriculum committee members or teachers with particular expertise in curriculum area and other teachers. And develop calendar skills and training components for monitoring development and implementation of curriculum.

• (Add items as appropriate.)

Step Two: Be an Instructional Resource for Your Staff

Box C.1   Rubric: Instructional Leadership Assessment and Plan of Improvement

Name _____ Grade _____

Peer Reviewer _____

(Please review syllabus for specific and general guidelines about assignments.)

• Overview of school and principal   _____ (10)

(Description of instructional leadership team's staffing and responsibilities, school size, schooling level)

- Assessment   _____ (30)

(Description specific to your situation, concrete examples, your words)

- Plan for improvement and development   _____ (35)

(Specific suggested activities for improvement and development for each descriptor as appropriate, relevance, thoroughness)

- Summary paragraph   _____ (15)

(Overall impressions, strengths and weaknesses of instructional leader, review of scoring)

- Writing mechanics, clarity of presentation   _____ (10)

(Editing, grammar, style, format, readability)

(A = 90 – 100; B = 80 – 89; C = 70 – 79)   *Total _____ (100)*

SOURCE: Reprinted by permission of ElizaBeth McCay.

References

Accelerated Schools Project. (2002). Located at the National Center for Accelerated Schools at the University of Connecticut at Storrs. Retrieved April 2002 from www.acceleratedschools.net/

Acheson, K. (1985). *The principal's role in instructional leadership.* Eugene: Oregon School Study Council, University of Oregon.

Acheson, K., & Smith, S. C. (1986). *It is time for principals to share the responsibility for instructional leadership with others.* Eugene: Oregon School Study Council, University of Oregon.

Ackerman, R. H., Donaldson, G. A., & van der Bogert, R. (1996). *Making sense as a school leader: Persisting questions, creative opportunities.* San Francisco: Jossey-Bass.

Ames, R. (1989, Fall). Feedback needed to create leadership teams. *Leadership and Learning Newsletter.* Urbana-Champaign: University of Illinois National Center for School Leadership.

Andrews, R. (1989). The Illinois principal as instructional leader: A concept and definition paper. *Illinois Principal, 20*(3), 4-12.

Andrews, R., & Soder, R. (1987). Principal leadership and student achievement. *Educational Leadership, 44*(6), 9-11.

Aristotle. (1933). *The metaphysics, books I-IX (Book I).* (H. Tredennick, Trans.). Cambridge, MA: Harvard University Press.

Arthur Andersen LLP. (1997). *Annual report on the Jersey City and Paterson Public Schools* (prepared for the New Jersey Legislature Joint Committee on the Public Schools). St. Charles, IL: Author.

Autry, J. (1991). *Love and profit: The art of caring leadership.* New York: William Morrow.

Barker, J. (1992). *Future edge: Discovering the new paradigms of success.* New York: William Morrow.

Barth, R. (1980). *Run school run.* Cambridge, MA: Harvard University Press.

Bass, B. M., & Stogdill, R. M. (1990). *Bass and Stogdill's handbook of leadership: Theory, research, and managerial applications.* New York: Free Press.

Bennis, W. (1989). *On becoming a leader.* Reading, MA: Addison-Wesley.

Bennis, W., & Nanus, B. (1985). *Leaders: The strategies for taking charge.* New York: Harper & Row.

Bird, T. D., & Little, J. W. (1985). *Instructional leadership in eight secondary schools. Final report.* Boulder, CO: Center for Action Research.

Blanchard, K. H., Zigarmi, P., & Zigarmi, D. (1985). *Leadership and the one-minute manager: Increasing effectiveness through situational leadership.* New York: William Morrow.

Bloom, B. S. (1980). The new direction in educational research: Alterable variables. *Phi Delta Kappan, 61*(6), 382-385.

Boyer, E. (1983). *High school: A report on secondary education in America.* New York: Harper & Row.

Bradley, A., & Olson, L. (1993, February 24). The balance of power. *Education Week,* p. 11.

Bransford, J. D., Brown, A. L., & Cocking, R. R. (Eds.). (2000). *How people learn: Brain, mind, experience, and school.* Washington, DC: National Academy Press.

Burns, J. M. (1978). *Leadership.* New York: Harper & Row.

Coalition of Essential Schools. (2002). Oakland, CA. Retrieved April 2002 from www.essentialschools.org/aboutus/aboutus.html

Comer School Development Program (2002). New Haven, CT. Retrieved April 2002 from www.med.yale.edu/comer/

Covey, S. R. (1989). *The seven habits of highly effective people: Restoring the character ethic.* New York: Simon & Schuster.

Deal, T. (1985). The symbolism of effective schools. *Elementary School Journal, 85*(5), 601-620.

Deal, T. (1986). Educational change: Revival tent, Tinker Toys, jungle, or carnival. In A. Lieberman (Ed.), *Rethinking school improvement: Research, craft, and concept* (pp. 115-128). New York: Teachers College Press.

Deal, T. E. (1987). The culture of schools. In L. T. Sheive & M. B. Schoenheit (Eds.), *Leadership: Examining the elusive* (pp. 3-15). Alexandria, VA: Association for Supervision & Curriculum Development.

Deal, T. E., & Kennedy, A. A. (1982). *Corporate cultures: The rites and rituals of corporate life.* Reading, MA: Addison-Wesley.

deGroat, A. F., & Thompson, G. G. (1949). A study of the distribution of teacher approval and disapproval among sixth grade pupils. *Journal of Experimental Education, 18,* 57-75.

Denning, S. (2000). *The springboard: How storytelling ignites action in knowledge-era organizations.* Portsmouth, NH: Butterworth-Heinemann.

DePree, M. (1989). *Leadership is an art.* New York: Doubleday.

Dobberteen, C. (1999). California School Recognition Program, 2000 Elementary School Application, La Mesa Dale Elementary School, La Mesa, CA. Unpublished document.

Dobberteen, C. (2000). Application for Title I Distinguished School, La Mesa Dale Elementary School, La Mesa, CA. Unpublished document.

Dobberteen, C. (2001). Second Annual Chase Change Award: Essay, La Mesa Dale Elementary School, La Mesa, CA. Unpublished document.

DuFour, R. P. (1991). *The principal as staff developer.* Bloomington, IN: National Education Service.

Drucker, P. (1990). *Managing the nonprofit organization: Principles and practices.* New York: HarperCollins.

Edison Schools (2002). New York. Retrieved April 27, 2002, from www.edisonschools.com/home/home.cfm

Educational Research Service. (2000). *The principal, keystone of a high-achieving school: Attracting and keeping the leaders we need.* Report prepared for the

National Association of Elementary School Principals and National Association of Secondary School Principals. Arlington, VA: Author.

Fink, E., & Resnick, L. (2001). Developing principals as instructional leaders. *Phi Delta Kappan, 82*(8), 598-606.

Fullan, M. (1992). *Successful school improvement: The implementation perspective and beyond.* Philadelphia: Open University Press.

Fullan, M. (1997). *What's worth fighting for in the principalship.* New York: Teachers College Press.

Fullan, M. G., & Hargreaves, A. (1991). *What's worth fighting for? Working together for your school.* Toronto, Canada: Ontario Public School Teachers Federation.

Garcia, A. (1986, November). Consensus decision-making promotes involvement, ownership, satisfaction. *NASSP Bulletin, 50*, p. 2.

Garfield, C. (1986). *Peak performers: The new heroes of American business.* New York: William Morrow.

Glickman, C. D. (1991). Pretending not to know what we know. *Educational Leadership, 48*(8), 4-10.

Glickman, C. D. (1993). *Renewing America's schools: A guide for school-based action.* San Francisco: Jossey-Bass.

Good, T. L., & Brophy, J. E. (1971). Analyzing classroom interaction: A more powerful alternative. *Educational Technology, 11*(10), 36-41.

Goodlad, J. I. (1984). *A place called school: Prospects for the future.* New York: McGraw-Hill.

Greenleaf, R. K. (1977). *Servant leadership: A journey into the nature of legitimate power and greatness.* New York: Paulist Press.

Guzzetti, B., & Martin, M. (1984). A comparative analysis of elementary and secondary principals' instructional leadership behavior. Boulder: University of Colorado. (ERIC Document Reproduction Service No. ED 245 399)

Hallinger, P., & Heck, R. (1996). Reassessing the principal's role in school effectiveness: A review of empirical research. *Educational Administration Quarterly, 32*(1), 5-44.

Hallinger, P., & Murphy, J. (1987). Assessing and developing principal instructional leadership. *Educational Leadership, 45*(1), 54-61.

Heifetz, R. A. (1994). *Leadership without easy answers.* Cambridge, MA: Belknap Press, Harvard University Press.

Holcomb, E. (1999). *Getting excited about data: How to combine people, passion, and proof.* Thousand Oaks, CA: Corwin.

Institute for Educational Leadership. (2000). *Leadership for school learning: Reinventing the principalship.* Washington, DC: Author.

Johnson, D. W., & Johnson, R. T. (1989). *Leading the cooperative school.* Edina, MN: Interaction Book Co.

Joyce, B., & Showers, B. (1995). *Student achievement through staff development.* New York: Longman.

Kanter, R. M. (1983). *The change masters: Innovation and entrepreneurship in the American corporation.* New York: Simon & Schuster.

Keller, B. (1998, November 11). Principal matters. *Education Week*, pp. 25-27.

Kelly, E. A. (Ed.). (1980). *Improving school climate: Leadership techniques for principals.* Reston, VA: National Association of Secondary Principals.

Kerman, S. (1979). Teacher expectations and student achievement. *Phi Delta Kappan, 60*(10), 716-718.

Kohl, H. (1998). *The discipline of hope: Learning from a lifetime of teaching.* New York: Simon & Schuster.

Kotter, J. P., & Heskett, J. L. (1992). *Corporate culture and performance.* New York: Free Press.

Krajewski, S. J. (1978, September). Secondary principals want to be instructional leaders. *Phi Delta Kappan,* pp. 65-69.

Labovitz, G., & Rosansky, V. (1997). *The power of alignment.* New York: John Wiley.

Lasley, T. J., & Wayson, W. W. (1982). Characteristics of schools with good discipline. *Educational Leadership, 40*(3), 28-31.

Leithwood, K., Aitken, R., & Jantzi, D. (2001). *Making schools smarter: A system for monitoring school and district progress.* Thousand Oaks, CA: Corwin.

Lezotte, L. W. (1992). *Creating the total quality effective school.* Okemos, MI: Effective Schools Products.

Lieberman, A. (1988). Expanding the leadership team. *Educational Leadership, 45*(5), 4-8.

Lightfoot, S. L. (1983). *The good high school.* New York: Basic Books.

Linn, E., & Barquet, N. (1992, Autumn). Assessing the tracking practices in your school. *Equity Coalition,* pp. 16-17.

Little (1985)

Little, J. W. (1987). Teachers as colleagues. In V. Richardson-Koehler (Ed.), *Educators' handbook: A research perspective* (pp. 419-518). New York: Longman.

Living Bible, The. (1971). I Corinthians 13:1. Wheaton, IL: Tyndale House.

Machiavelli, N. (1985). *The prince.* (H. C. Mansfield, Trans.). Chicago: University of Chicago Press. (Original work published in 1695.)

Maeroff, G. (1993). Building teams to rebuild schools. *Phi Delta Kappan, 74*(7), 512-519.

Mahaffy, J. E. (1988). *Collegial support system: A process model draft.* Booklet prepared for the Northwest Regional Educational Laboratory. Portland, OR: Northwest Regional Educational Laboratory.

Manna, P. (1999, November 17). Hooked on a feeling. *Education Week.* Retrieved April 25, 2002, from www.edweek.com/ew/ewstory.cfm

Matusak, L. R., & Young, A. (1997). *Finding your voice: Learning to lead—anywhere you want to make a difference.* San Francisco: Jossey-Bass.

McEwan, E. K. (1997). *Leading your team to excellence: How to make quality decisions.* Thousand Oaks, CA: Corwin.

McEwan, E. K. (1998). *When kids say no to school: Helping children at risk of failure, refusal, or dropping out.* Wheaton, IL: Harold Shaw.

McEwan, E. K. (2001). *Ten traits of highly effective teachers: How to hire, mentor and coach successful teachers.* Thousand Oaks, CA: Corwin.

McEwan, E. K. (2002). *Teach them all to read: Catching the kids who fall through the cracks.* Thousand Oaks, CA: Corwin.

McEwan, E. K., & Damer, M. (2000). *Managing unmanageable students: Practical tips for administrators.* Thousand Oaks, CA: Corwin.

McKechnie, J. L. (Ed.). (1983). *Webster's new universal unabridged dictionary* (2nd ed.). New York: Simon & Schuster.

Mendez-Morse, S. (2001). *Leadership characteristics that facilitate school change.* Austin, TX: Southwest Educational Development Laboratory.

Montgomery, B. (1961). *The path to leadership.* New York: Putnam.

Morris, V., Crowson, R. L., Hurwitz, E., Jr., & Porter-Gehrie, C. (1982, June). The urban principal: Middle manager in the educational bureaucracy. *Phi Delta Kappan, 63*(10), 689-692.

National Association of Elementary School Principals. (2001). *Leading learning communities: Standards for what principals should know and be able to do.* Alexandria, VA: Author.

National Association of Secondary School Principals. (2001). *Priorities and barriers in high school leadership: A survey of principals.* Reston, VA: Author.

National Research Council. (2000). *How people learn: Brain, mind, experience, and school.* Washington, DC: National Academy Press.

Neuhauser, P. C. (1993). *Corporate legends and lore: The power of storytelling.* New York: McGraw-Hill.

Northwest Educational Cooperative. (1985). *Principals who produce results: How they think; what they do.* Arlington Heights, IL: Author.

Northwest Regional Educational Laboratory. (1984). *Effective schooling practices: A research synthesis.* Portland, OR: Author.

Oakes, J. (1985). *Keeping track: How schools structure inequality.* New Haven, CT: Yale University Press.

Olson, L. (2000, January 12). Policy focus converges on leadership. *Education Week.* Retrieved April 25, 2002, from www.edweek.com/ew/ewstory.cfm

Oxnard High School. (2001). Retrieved April 25, 2002, from www.ouhsd.k12.ca.us/sites/ohs/ohs.htm

Pajak, E. (1993). Change and continuity in supervision and leadership. In G. Cawelti (Ed.), *Challenges and achievements of American education* (pp. 178-188). Alexandria, VA: Association for Supervision & Curriculum Development.

Perkins, D. (1992). *Smart schools: From training memories to educating minds.* New York: Free Press.

Persell, C., & Cookson, P. (1982). The effective principal in action. In National Association of Secondary School Principals (Ed.), *The effective principal: A research summary* (pp. 22-29). Reston, VA: Editor.

Peters, T., & Austin, N. (1985). *A passion for excellence: The leadership difference.* New York: Random House.

Popcorn, F., & Hanft, A. (2001). *Dictionary of the future.* New York: Hyperion.

Portin, B., & Williams, B. (1996). *The changing role of the principal: A survey of Washington State's principals and assistant principals.* Olympia, WA: Association of Washington School Principals.

Powell, A. G., Farrar, E., & Cohen, D. K. (1985). *The shopping mall high school: Winners and losers in the educational marketplace.* Boston: Houghton Mifflin.

Public Agenda. (2001). *Trying to stay ahead of the game: Superintendents and principals talk about school leadership.* New York: Author.

Raywid, M. A., Tesconie, C., & Warren, D. (1985). *Pride and promise: Schools of excellence for all people.* Westbury, NY: American Educational Studies Association.

Richard, A. (2000, November 1). Panel calls for fresh look at duties facing principals. *Education Week.* Retrieved April 25, 2002, from www.edweek.com/ew/ewstory.cfm

Rogers, C. (1974). In retrospect—forty-six years. *American Psychologist, 29*(2), 115-123.

Roper, S. S., & Hoffman, D. E. (1986). *Collegial support for professional improvement: The Stanford Collegial Evaluation Program.* Eugene: Oregon School Study Council, University of Oregon.

Rosenbaum, J. E. (1980). Social implications of educational grouping. In D. C. Berliner (Ed.), *Review of Research in Education* (pp. 361-401). Itasca, IL: American Educational Research Association.

Rosenshine, D., & Berliner, D. (1980). Academic engaged time. *British Journal of Teacher Education, 6,* 3-16.

Rutherford, W. (1985). School principals as effective leaders. *Phi Delta Kappan, 67*(1), 31-34.

Sagor, R. D. (1992). Three principals who make a difference. *Educational Leadership, 49*(5), 13-18.

Saphier, J., & Gower, R. (1997). *The skillful teacher: Building your teaching skills.* Acton: MA: Research for Better Teaching.

Saphier, J., & King, M. (1985). Good seeds grow in strong cultures. *Educational Leadership, 42*(6), 67-74.

Sarason, S. (1990). *The predictable failure of educational reform: Can we change course before it's too late?* San Francisco: Jossey-Bass.

Scheidecker, D., & Freeman, W. (1999). *Bringing out the best in kids: How legendary teachers motivate kids.* Thousand Oaks, CA: Corwin.

Schlechty, P. C. (1990). *Schools for the 21st century: Leadership imperatives for educational reform.* San Francisco: Jossey-Bass.

Schmoker, M. (1999). *Results: The key to continuous school improvement.* Alexandria, VA: Association for Supervision & Curriculum Development.

Schwahn, C. J., & Spady, W. G. (1998). *Total leaders: Applying the best future-focused change strategies to education.* Arlington, VA: Association for Supervision & Curriculum Development.

Sergiovanni, T. (1984). Leadership and excellence in schooling. *Educational Leadership, 41*(5), 4, 6-13.

Sergiovanni, T. (1991). *The principalship: A reflective practice perspective* (2nd ed.). Boston: Allyn & Bacon.

Sergiovanni, T. (1992). Why we should seek substitutes for leadership. *Educational Leadership, 49*(5), 41-45.

Sergiovanni, T. (2001). *The principalship: A reflective practice perspective* (4th ed.). Boston: Allyn & Bacon.

Slavin, R. E, & Madden, N. A. (2001). *One million children: Success for all.* Thousand Oaks, CA: Corwin.

Smith, W. F., & Andrews, R. (1989). *Instructional leadership: How principals make a difference.* Alexandria, VA: Association for Supervision & Curriculum Development.

Spady, W. (1992, July). Paper presented at the Suburban Superintendents' Conference, Traverse City, Michigan.

Sparks, D. (1993, Winter). The professional development of principals: A conversation with Roland Barth. *Journal of Staff Development, 14,* 17-19.

Stallings, J. A. (1980). Allocated academic learning time revisited, or beyond time on task. *Educational Researcher, 9,* 9-11.

Stallings, J. (1989, August). Paper presented at the National School Improvement Symposium, Farmington, Connecticut.

Stotsky, S. (Ed.). (2000). *What's at stake in the K-12 standards wars: A primer for educational policy makers.* New York: Peter Lang Publishing.

Tannenbaum, R., Weschler, I. R., & Massarik, F. (1961). *Leadership and organization.* New York: McGraw-Hill.

Troen, V., & Boles, K. (1994, February). A time to lead. *Teacher Magazine,* pp. 40-41.

U.S. Commission on Civil Rights. (1973). *Teachers and students: Differences in teacher interaction with Mexican American and Anglo students (Report V: Mexican American education study).* Washington, DC: U.S. Government Printing Office.

Weber, J. R. (1987). *Instructional leadership: A composite working model.* Eugene, OR: ERIC Clearinghouse on Educational Management.

Weick, K. (1982). Administering education in loosely coupled schools. *Phi Delta Kappan, 63*(10), 673-676.

Wiggins, G. (1993). *Assessing student performance: Exploring the purpose and limits of testing.* San Francisco: Jossey-Bass.

Index

**CORWIN
PRESS**

The Corwin Press logo—a raven striding across an open book—represents the happy union of courage and learning. We are a professional-level publisher of books and journals for K-12 educators, and we are committed to creating and providing resources that embody these qualities. Corwin's motto is "Success for All Learners."